Specification lists

AQA Business Studies

MODULE	SPECIFICATION TOPIC	CHAPTER REFERENCE	STUDIED IN CLASS	REVISED	PRACTICE QUESTIONS
Module 1 **(M1)** *Marketing and accounting and finance*	Market analysis	7.2			
	Marketing strategy	7.1–7.3			
	Marketing planning	7.1–7.3			
	Costs, profit, contribution and break-even	5.1–5.4			
	Company accounts	5.2			
	Budgeting	5.4			
	Cost and profit centres	5.4			
Module 2 **(M2)** *People and operations management*	Management structure and organisation	3.1, 3.2, 6.1			
	Motivation	6.4			
	Human resource management	6.1–6.3			
	Productive efficiency	3.4, 3.5, 8.1–8.3			
	Controlling operations	8.2, 8.3, 8.4			
	Lean production	8.1			
Module 3 **(M3)** *External influences and objectives and strategy*	Economic	1.3, 1.4, 4.1			
	Governmental	4.2, 6.3			
	Social and other	4.4			
	Opportunities and constraints	2.2, 2.3, 4.3			
	Starting a small firm	2.2, 4.2			
	Business objectives	1.1, 1.2, 1.4, 2.1–2.5			
	Business strategy	1.3, 1.4, 2.2–2.5			

Examination analysis

The specification for the AS examination (5131) comprises three tests.

Unit 1	Two compulsory stimulus-response questions based on AS Module 1 content	1 hr test	30%
Unit 2	A number of compulsory questions based on a pre-issued case study (common to Unit 3)	1 hr test	30%
Unit 3	A number of compulsory questions based on a pre-issued case study (common to Unit 2)	1 hr test	40%

Edexcel Business Studies

MODULE	SPECIFICATION TOPIC	CHAPTER REFERENCE	STUDIED IN CLASS	REVISED	PRACTICE QUESTIONS
Module 1 (M1) Business structures, objectives and external influences	Structure of business	1.1, 1.2, 1.4, 2.1–2.4			
	Business objectives and stakeholders	2.5			
	Economic influences	1.3, 1.4, 4.1, 4.2			
	Legal, political and social influences	4.3, 4.4			
	Internal organisation	3.1, 3.2, 3.4, 3.5			
	Communication in business	3.3			
	Motivation in business	6.1, 6.2, 6.4			
Module 2 (M2) Marketing and production	Nature and role of marketing	7.1			
	Market research	7.2			
	Product	7.3			
	Pricing, promotion and place	7.3			
	Operational efficiency	8.1–8.3			
	Quality	8.4			
Module 3 (M3) Financial management	Financial accounts	5.1–5.3			
	Budgeting	5.4			
	Cost classification and analysis	5.2, 5.4			

Examination analysis

The specification for the AS examination comprises three unit tests, all of which are based on the same pre-issued case study.

Unit 1	Compulsory structured questions based on AS Unit 1 content	1 hr test	30%
Unit 2	Unseen case study based on AS Unit 2 content	1 hr test	40%
Unit 3	Compulsory structured questions based on AS Unit 3 content	1 hr test	30%

OCR Business Studies

MODULE	SPECIFICATION TOPIC	CHAPTER REFERENCE	STUDIED IN CLASS	REVISED	PRACTICE QUESTIONS
Unit 2871 (M1) Businesses, their objectives and environment	The nature of business	1.2, 1.3, 2.2–2.4			
	Classification of business	1.2, 2.1			
	Objectives	2.2–2.5			
	Strategic planning	2.5, 7.1			
	External influences	1.1, 1.3, 1.4, 4.2–4.3			
	Other influences	4.4			
Units 2872 (M2) **and 2873 (M3)** Business decisions; business behaviour	Marketing	7.1			
	The market	1.3, 7.1			
	Market research	7.2			
	Marketing planning	7.1–7.3			
	Accounting and finance	5.1			
	Budgets	5.4			
	Cash flow	5.4			
	Costs	5.1–5.4			
	Investment decisions	5.3			
	Final accounts	5.2			
	People in organisations	6.2, 6.3			
	Human resource planning	6.1			
	Motivation and leadership	6.4			
	Management structure	3.1, 3.2			
	Operations management	8.2			
	Operational efficiency	3.4, 3.5			
	Organising production	8.1			
	Quality	8.4			
	Stock control	8.3			

Examination analysis

The specification for the AS examination comprises three unit tests.

Unit 2871	Five compulsory questions based on a pre-issued case study	1 hr test	30%
Unit 2872	Four compulsory data-response questions	45 min test	30%
Unit 2873	Four compulsory questions based on a pre-issued case study	1 hr 15 min test	40%

WJEC Business Studies

MODULE	SPECIFICATION TOPIC	CHAPTER REFERENCE	STUDIED IN CLASS	REVISED	PRACTICE QUESTIONS
Unit BS 1 section 3.1 (M1) Objectives and the business environment	Needs and wants	1.1			
	Public and private sectors	1.2, 2.2–2.4			
	Goods and services	1.2, 1.3, 2.1			
	Industrial sectors	1.2			
	Types of business organisation	2.1–2.4			
	Business objectives and planning	2.2–2.5, 3.1			
	Organisational structure	3.1, 3.2			
	External influences	4.1–4.4			
Unit BS 2 section 3.2 (M2) Marketing	Nature and role of marketing	7.1			
	Market research	7.2			
	The marketing plan	7.3			
	Forecasting	7.2			
	International marketing	1.4, 7.1			
Unit BS 2 section 3.3 (M3) Accounting and finance	Sources of business finance	5.3			
	Budgeting and cash flow	5.4			
	Final accounts	5.1, 5.2			
	Costs and break-even analysis	5.4			
Unit BS 3 section 3.4 (M4) People in organisations	Human resources	6.1			
	Motivation	6.4			
	Employer/employee relations	6.2, 6.3			
	Organisations and management structures	3.2, 6.1			
Unit BS 3 section 3.5 (M5) Operations management	Operational efficiency	3.4, 3.5, 8.1–8.3			
	Quality	8.4			
	Technology	8.2			
	Business location	3.5, 8.1			

Examination analysis

The specification for the AS examination comprises three unit tests.

Unit BS1	Short-answer and stimulus-response questions based on AS section 3.1	1 hr test	40%
Unit BS2	One compulsory stimulus-response question on AS section 3.2, and one on AS section 3.3	1 hr test	30%
Unit BS3	One compulsory stimulus-response question on AS section 3.4, and one on AS section 3.5	1 hr test	30%

NICCEA Business Studies

MODULE	SPECIFICATION TOPIC	CHAPTER REFERENCE	STUDIED IN CLASS	REVISED	PRACTICE QUESTIONS
Module 1 (M1) Objectives and the business environment	Sectors of the economy	1.2, 2.2–2.4			
	Business ownership in Northern Ireland	2.2–2.4			
	Small firms, multinationals, buyouts	2.3, 3.1			
	External environment	1.1, 1.4, 4.1, 4.3, 4.4			
	Government assistance	4.2			
	Population	3.5, 4.4			
	Planning, objectives and decision-making	2.5, 4.2			
Module 2 (M2) People in organisations and accounting and finance	Recruitment and selection	6.2			
	Employment	6.1, 6.3			
	Leadership and management	6.4			
	Delegation and decentralisation	3.1, 3.2, 6.4			
	Training	6.2			
	Employment legislation	6.3			
	Sources of finance	5.3			
	Costs, revenue, profit	5.1, 5.2, 5.4			
	Break-even analysis	5.4			
	Budgeting and cash-flow	5.4			
	Final accounts	5.2			
Module 3 (M3) Marketing and operations management	Market research	7.2			
	Demand and supply	1.3, 7.1			
	Marketing strategy	7.1–7.3			
	International marketing	1.4, 7.1			
	Operations management	8.1–8.3			
	Production	8.1			
	Growth of firms	3.4			
	Monopolies and mergers	3.4, 3.5, 4.3			
	Quality	8.4			

Examination analysis

The specification for the AS examination comprises three unit tests.

Unit 1	Two compulsory stimulus-response questions based on AS Module 1 content	1 hr 40 min test	40%
Unit 2	Two compulsory stimulus-response questions based on AS Module 2 content	1 hr 20 min test	30%
Unit 3	Two compulsory stimulus-response questions based on AS Module 3 content	1 hr 20 min test	30%

AS/A2 Level Business Studies courses

AS and A2

All Business Studies courses being studied from September 2000 are in two parts, with three separate modules in AS and three in A2. Students first study the AS (Advanced Subsidiary) course. Some will then go on to study the second part of the A Level course, called A2. Advanced Subsidiary is assessed at the standard expected halfway through an A Level course: i.e., between GCSE and Advanced GCE. This means that the new AS and A2 courses are _designed_ so that difficulty steadily increases:

- AS Business Studies builds from GCSE Business Studies
- A2 Business Studies builds from AS Business Studies

How will you be tested?

Assessment units

For AS Business Studies, you will be tested by three assessment units. For the full A Level in Business Studies, you will take a further three units. AS Business Studies forms 50% of the assessment weighting for the full A Level.

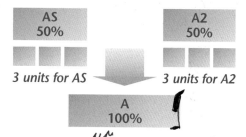

Each unit can normally be taken in either January or June. Alternatively, you can study the whole course before taking any of the unit tests. There is a lot of flexibility about when exams can be taken, and the diagram below shows just some of the ways that the assessment units may be taken for AS and A Level Business Studies.

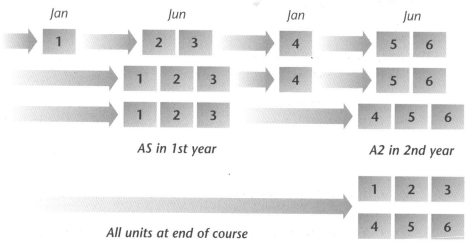

If you are disappointed with a module result, you can _resit_ each module once. You will need to be very careful about when you take up a resit opportunity because you will have only one chance to improve your mark. The higher mark counts.

A2 and Synoptic assessment

After having studied AS Business Studies, you may wish to continue studying Business Studies to A Level. For this you will need to take three further units of Business Studies at A2. Similar assessment arrangements apply except some units, those that draw together different parts of the course in a 'synoptic' assessment, have to be assessed at the end of the course. Synoptic assessment is likely to test your ability to apply knowledge, understanding and skills you have learnt throughout the course, and to make business decisions and/or solve business problems.

Key skills

It is important that you develop your key skills throughout your AS and A2 courses. These are important skills that you need whatever you do beyond AS and A2 Levels. To gain the key skills qualification, which is equivalent to an AS Level, you will need to collect evidence together in a 'portfolio' to show that you have attained Level 3 in Communication, Application of number and Information technology. You will also need to take a formal testing in each key skill.

It is a worthwhile qualification, as it demonstrates your ability to put your ideas across to other people, collect data and use up-to-date technology in your work.

You will have many opportunities during AS Business Studies to develop your key skills. Business Studies specifications also provide opportunities for you to produce evidence for assessing the key skills of improving own learning and performance, Working with others, and Problem-solving.

What skills will I need?

Business Studies A Level specifications encourage you to:

*   develop a critical understanding of organisations, their internal structure and the external environment in which they operate;
*   study and analyse business from a number of different perspectives;
*   acquire a range of skills, including decision-making and problem-solving;
*   be aware of changes and developments in business life and practice.

For AS Business Studies, you will be tested by assessment objectives: these are the skills and abilities that you should have acquired by studying the course, and have an equal weighting for the whole A Level qualification. These are the four assessment objectives for AS Business Studies.

1   Demonstrate knowledge and understanding of the specified content.
2   Apply knowledge and critical understanding to problems and issues arising from both familiar and unfamiliar situations.
3   Analyse problems, issues and situations.
4   Evaluate, distinguish between fact and opinion, and assess information from a variety of sources.

Your final A Level grade depends on the extent to which you meet these assessment objectives. This is explained further on page 15.

Exam technique

Links from GCSE

Advanced Subsidiary Business Studies builds from GCSE Business Studies. This study guide has been written so that you will be able to tackle AS Business Studies from a GCSE Business Studies background.

The study guide includes important business concepts and information. If you have not studied GCSE Business Studies before, you will still be able to study for AS Level using this book.

What are examiners looking for?

Examiners use instructions to help you to decide the length and depth of your answer.

State, define, list, outline

These key words require short, concise answers, often recall of material that you have memorised.

Explain, describe, discuss

Some reasoning or some reference to theory is needed, depending on the context. Explaining and discussing require you to give a more detailed answer than when you are asked to 'describe' something.

Apply

Here, you must make sure that you relate your answer to the given situation (this is always good practice in Business Studies exams).

Evaluate

You are required to provide full and detailed arguments, often 'for' and 'against', to show your depth of understanding.

Calculate

A numerical answer is required here.

Some dos and don'ts

Dos

Do answer the question.

- No credit can be given for good Business Studies knowledge that is not relevant to the question.

Do use the mark allocation to guide how much you write.

- Writing more than necessary will not result in extra marks.

Do use real-life business-based examples in your answers.

- These often help illustrate your level of knowledge.

Do write legibly.

- An examiner cannot give marks if the answer cannot be read.

Do use correct 'business language'.

- Marks will be lost if you fail to use terms appropriately.

Don'ts

Don't fill up blank spaces on the exam paper.

- If you write too much on one question, you may run out of time to answer some of the others.

Don't contradict yourself.

- Present reasoned arguments for and against.

Don't spend too much time on a part that you find difficult.

- Exam time is limited, and you can always return to the difficult part if you have enough time at the end of the exam.

What grade do you want?

Everyone would like to improve their grades but you will only manage this with a lot of hard work and determination. Your final A Level grade depends on the extent to which you meet the assessment objectives listed on page 10. The hints below offer advice on how to improve your grade.

For a grade A

You have to:

- show in-depth knowledge and critical understanding of a wide range of business theory and concepts;
- apply this to familiar and unfamiliar situations, problems and issues, using appropriate numerical and non-numerical techniques;
- evaluate effectively evidence and arguments; and
- make reasoned judgements in presenting appropriate conclusions.

You have to be a very good all-rounder to achieve a grade A. The exams and coursework test all areas of the syllabus, and any weaknesses in your understanding of Business Studies will be found out.

For a grade C

You have to have a good understanding of the aspects shown in the grade A bullet-points, but you will have weaknesses in some of these areas. To improve, you will need to work hard to overcome these weaknesses, and also make sure that you have an efficient and effective exam technique.

As a rough guide you will need to score an average of between 50% and 60% for a grade C, and over 75% for a grade A..

average	80%	70%	60%	50%	40%
grade	A	B	C	D	E

Four steps to successful revision

Step 1: Understand

- Study the topic to be learned slowly. Make sure you understand the logic or important concepts
- Mark up the text if necessary – underline, highlight and make notes
- Re-read each paragraph slowly.

GO TO STEP 2

Step 2: Summarise

- Now make your own revision note summary:
  What is the main idea, theme or concept to be learned?
  What are the main points? How does the logic develop?
  Ask questions: Why? How? What next?
- Use bullet points, mind maps, patterned notes
- Link ideas with mnemonics, mind maps, crazy stories
- Note the title and date of the revision notes
  (e.g. Business Studies: Marketing, 3rd March)
- Organise your notes carefully and keep them in a file.

This is now in **short term memory**. You will forget 80% of it if you do not go to Step 3.
GO TO STEP 3, but first take a 10 minute break.

Step 3: Memorise

- Take 25 minute learning 'bites' with 5 minute breaks
- After each 5 minute break test yourself:
  Cover the original revision note summary
  Write down the main points
  Speak out loud (record on tape)
  Tell someone else
  Repeat many times.

The material is well on its way to **long term memory**.
You will forget 40% if you do not do step 4. **GO TO STEP 4**

Step 4: Track/Review

- Create a Revision Diary (one A4 page per day)
- Make a revision plan for the topic, e.g. 1 day later, 1 week later, 1 month later.
- Record your revision in your Revision Diary, e.g.
  Business Studies: Marketing, 3rd March 25 minutes
  Business Studies: Marketing, 5th March 15 minutes
  Business Studies: Marketing, 3rd April 15 minutes
  ... and then at monthly intervals.

Chapter 1

The external environment

The following topics are covered in this chapter:

- Types of economy
- Sectors of the UK economy
- Markets
- International trade

1.1 Types of economy

After studying this section you should be able to:

- define in your own words 'market', 'command' and 'mixed' economies
- describe the key features of each of the market and command systems
- explain why mixed economies are found in practice

The market economy

AQA	M3
EDEXCEL	M1
OCR	M1
WJEC	M1
NICCEA	M1

Economies differ in the way that they allocate scarce economic resources to competing uses. As production takes place, the goods and services made consume (use up) economic resources. These resources have costs associated with them. An accountant measures the **financial** cost of these resources: for example, the cost of paying wages, or the cost of interest on borrowed money. An economist considers the **opportunity cost** of production: resources that are allocated to one use cannot be used for something else at the same time. Land being used for agriculture cannot also be built upon; labour employed in making cars cannot also work at the same time in the retail industry.

> **KEY POINT**
>
> All economies must find answers to these questions:
> **What** do we produce?
> **How** do we produce it?
> **For whom** do we produce?

Firms located in market economies

> Changing prices give **signals**, and act as **incentives**, to buyers and sellers. For example, increased petrol prices signal lower car sales to vehicle manufacturers, and act as an incentive for people to use public transport.

In a true market economy (**free enterprise**), resources are privately owned. Production decisions are made by **entrepreneurs** and private individuals, and not by the state on behalf of its people. The **profit motive** is important, affecting demand, supply, and price (see page 24). The **price mechanism** allocates scarce resources, through changes in the price of these resources.

- The market economy is **efficient** in producing and allocating resources – but few 'perfectly competitive' markets exist, and so collusion between producers, incomplete price knowledge by consumers, restrictions on entry to new firms, and taxes/subsidies limit economic efficiency in practice.

- **Decentralised** decision-making should reduce bureaucracy ('red tape') for firms – but centralisation and bureaucracy may still exist (e.g. to control cartels, producers who ignore laws, etc.).

> Greater concern over environmental issues – considering not only financial costs ('price') but also social ones – is a good example of how the price mechanism can be distorted in practice.

- **Consumer sovereignty**: producers must satisfy their customers in order to make profits, and so the consumer influences what is produced – but the price mechanism and profit motive may result in social judgements being ignored, and the state must still intervene to ensure that non-profitable services (e.g. universal health care, defence) are provided.

The command, or planned, economy

AQA	M3
EDEXCEL	M1
OCR	M1
WJEC	M1
NICCEA	M1

A centrally planned, 'command', economy is the opposite form of economy. Although largely discredited in the West, in theory a planned economy can allocate resources as efficiently as a market one. Real-life command economies, such as those once widely found in Eastern Europe, concentrate on the **central control** of what is produced, how it is distributed, and at what price.

In recent years, many countries with planned economies have switched towards greater use of the price mechanism; examples include China, Russia and East European ex-communist countries.

Firms located in command economies

- **All costs are considered**, the central planning authority taking into account social and other costs not easily measured in financial terms – as a result, firms find market forces less of an influence.

- **Public goods** are provided, being made on the basis of need rather than profit – though since producers are not rewarded to the same extent there is a lack of this incentive, and therefore little encouragement to innovate and be efficient. Because prices are less influenced by demand/supply interaction, there are fewer price signals for producers: production targets have to be met, with the economy experiencing surpluses or shortages because of planning imperfections.

The mixed economy

AQA	M3
EDEXCEL	M1
OCR	M1
WJEC	M1
NICCEA	M1

Two sectors – **public** and **private** – exist in a mixed economy. The distinction between these sectors is based on **ownership** (see page 32), as well as on how resources are allocated. In practice, a wider range of goods and services is likely to be found in mixed economies. Both sectors may produce the same item: for example, health services in the UK are provided by organisations in both public (the NHS) and private (e.g. BUPA) sectors.

Throughout much of the last 20 years, the UK has seen a growth of the private sector at the expense of the public sector, with the **privatisation** of many public sector organisations (see page 41) having taken place.

> Both 'pure' market and planned economies do not exist in practice, and countries have a mixed economy to allocate their scarce resources.
>
> **KEY POINT**

Progress check

1 (a) Define the term 'opportunity cost'.
 (b) Illustrate how opportunity cost might affect an entrepreneur.

2 What do these terms mean, and how do they relate to economic systems?
 (a) free enterprise; (b) cartels; (c) bureaucracy.

1 (a) It is the cost of an opportunity forgone; resources used in one area cannot be used in another.
(b) The entrepreneur may only have money for a new van or a new machine: the opportunity cost of the van is the postponed purchase of the machine.
2 (a) Free enterprise is associated with market economies and the profit motive, i.e. when firms operate in an economy free from government interference.
(b) A number of market-economy producers controlling output to keep prices and profits higher than they would otherwise be. Cartels are controlled by law.
(c) More widely known as 'red tape', bureaucracy is particularly associated with planned economies due to the over-centralisation of government control.

1.2 Sectors of the UK economy

After studying this section you should be able to:

- *define in your own words the three production sectors in the UK economy*
- *give at least one UK-based example of each*
- *explain reasons for the trend towards a tertiary economy in the UK*

The sectors

AQA	M3
EDEXCEL	M1
OCR	M1
WJEC	M1
NICCEA	M1

Production is classified under three headings. These are:

- **Primary**: the primary sector consists of **extractive** industries such as fishing, forestry, farming, mining and quarrying.

- **Secondary**: the secondary sector – often described as 'industry' – consists of firms involved with **manufacturing** and **construction**.

- **Tertiary**: the tertiary sector contains organisations supplying services, both commercial services such as banking, finance and retailing, as well as direct service providers, e.g. health, education.

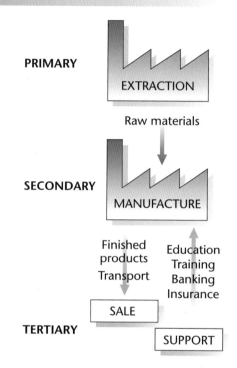

The UK economy

AQA	M3
EDEXCEL	M1
OCR	M1
WJEC	M1
NICCEA	M1

Figure 1.1 illustrates the change in the relative importance of these three sectors in the UK economy.

	Males (%)		Females (%)	
	1981	*1998*	*1981*	*1998*
Primary				
Agriculture	2	2	1	1
Secondary				
Manufacturing	33	25	18	10
Construction	8	8	1	1
Tertiary				
Distribution, hotels, catering and repairs	16	20	25	26
Financial and business services	10	16	12	19
Transport and communication	9	9	3	3
Other services	22	20	40	40
All jobs (=100%) (millions)	12.6	11.7	9.3	11.5

Figure 1.1 *Employee jobs, by gender and industry, in the UK*   Source: ONS (1999)

The table shows that a third of all male employee jobs were in manufacturing in 1981, compared with only a quarter in 1998. Although only one in ten male employee jobs was in financial and business services in 1981, by 1998 the same area accounted for one in six male jobs. There is a similar increase in female employee jobs, from approximately one in eight (1981) to one in five (1998). A substantial growth in the total number of women employed can be seen. This is partly as a result of the increase in part-time working (see page 95). These changes affect firms' **organisational culture and strategy**, and how they **manage change**.

> More people now work in call centres than in factories or coal mines.

The statistics show that manufacturing industry has declined in relative importance in the UK in recent years. This **de-industrialisation** reflects a long-term move towards tertiary production. In the first Industrial Revolution, many workers moved from the country to the towns, and changed to secondary production. The trend away from agriculture and extraction has continued, together with a further shift from secondary to tertiary. This is typical of other developed Western economies, whereas a number of developing economies are still experiencing a major shift from primary to secondary production.

> Output of the post and telecommunications (tertiary) sector grew 50% from 1995 to 1999, largely due to internet and mobile 'phone usage.

KEY POINT

Reasons for de-industrialisation in the UK include: increasing substitution of capital for labour (due to technological developments in production) in both primary and secondary sectors; the fall in the UK's competitiveness in secondary production, leading to more manufactured goods being imported; and the birth of newly industrialised competitor economies, such as the 'tiger economies' of the eastern Pacific rim (e.g. Taiwan, South Korea).

The information in Figure 1.2 below suggests that this trend is likely to continue.

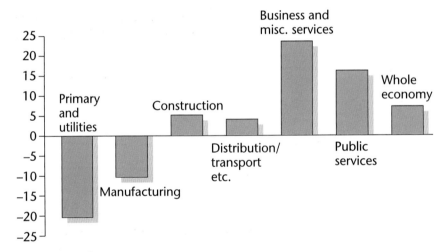

Figure 1.2 *Sectoral employment projections, percentage change, 1991–2000*
Source: Department for Education and Employment, 1996

Progress check

1 Give ONE example of a business in each of the three sectors.

2 (a) What do these terms mean, and how do they relate to classifying production? (i) de-industrialisation; (ii) extractive industry; (iii) tertiary. (b) Give an illustration for each term above.

1 Primary – a local farm; secondary – a car manufacturer; tertiary – a bank.

2 (a) (i) De-industrialisation refers to the trend away from manufacturing and construction industries towards the service sector.
(ii) An extractive industry removes value from the land (including the sea).
(iii) Tertiary is the service sector of the UK economy, which nowadays represents about 70% of the workforce.
(b) (i) The collapse in the UK of the traditional 'heavy engineering' industries such as steel (e.g. West Midlands) and shipbuilding (e.g. North-East England).
(ii) Mining, quarrying and fishing.
(iii) The growth in financial services.

1.3 Markets

After studying this section you should be able to:

- apply the fundamental laws of demand and supply to a firm's situation
- outline possible causes of a shift in the demand or supply curve
- explain the relevance to firms of price elasticity, income elasticity and cross-elasticity of demand

Markets and demand

AQA	M1, M3
EDEXCEL	M1
OCR	M1
WJEC	M1
NICCEA	M3

A market is a meeting of buyers and sellers, where goods/services are exchanged for other goods and services. It is therefore a system of exchange based on demand, supply and price. The exchange is normally indirect, the items being exchanged for money, which is used later to buy other items. Money acts as a medium of exchange and a measure of value: it is also a store of value.

> A **consumer market** buys and sells consumer goods.
>
> An **industrial market** buys and sells producer goods.

KEY POINT

The fundamental law of demand is:

price ↑ = quantity demanded ↓; price ↓ = quantity demanded ↑

If the demand for a firm's products is to be **effective**, it must be backed by money and by a willingness to buy. When a demand curve is plotted to show consumer behaviour in a single market, it appears as in Figure 1.3.

> The graph shows that 30,000 items are demanded when the price is £10. If the price falls to £5, quantity demanded will increase to 40,000.

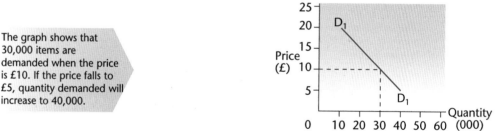

Figure 1.3 The demand curve

The curve is constructed from the individual demand curves of all consumers in the market. Its gradient varies according to the **elasticity of demand** (see page 24) for the item, the downward-sloping nature confirming that consumers demand more of the item as its price falls. Movements along the demand curve are due solely to price changes for the product, and are called **changes in quantity demanded**. The demand curve itself does not change position on the graph.

Shifts in the demand curve

Shifts in demand result in the demand curve moving position. These shifts will move the demand curve either to the right (Figure 1.4) or to the left (Figure 1.5).

> Figure 1.4 shows that the increase in demand (D$_2$) at a price of £10 is from 30,000 to 35,000. Figure 1.5 shows the decrease in demand (D$_3$) at the same price is from 30,000 to 25,000.

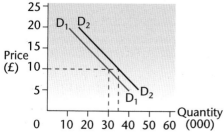

Figure 1.4 Increase in demand

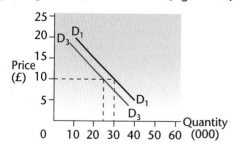

Figure 1.5 Decrease in demand

> Changes in demand are different from changes in quantity demanded.

Shifts in the demand curve are due to changes in:

Taste or fashion

Often associated with youth-influenced markets and trends, e.g. fashions in clothing, toys for Christmas. Also found when health-related information is made available on certain foodstuffs or other products, e.g. the apparent dangers of tobacco, or benefits of 'low-fat' varieties of products.

Price of substitutes

Many products have close substitutes: foodstuffs (e.g. different meats), branded products (e.g. soaps, washing-up liquids). A price increase for one good may increase demand for its substitute: the substitute's demand curve moves to the right even though its price has not altered.

Price of jointly-demanded products

With products having a joint demand, e.g. vehicles and petrol, DVD players and discs, a change in the price of one will affect the demand for its joint product.

Income

> Disposable income is affected by government direct and indirect taxation policies, and/or changes in employment and wage levels (e.g. creation of the National Minimum Wage).

An increase in disposable income may move a product's demand curve to the right, because consumers can now afford more of it. Increases in income might, in some cases, decrease demand (e.g. car manufacturers gain if 'inferior goods' such as public transport are replaced by the 'superior' substitute of private cars). The level of disposable income in business is also relevant, since firms create demand for labour and capital.

Innovation

New goods and services influence the demand for products currently on the market, e.g. technological innovations such as DVD players affecting the demand for VHS and CD players.

Population

Changes in population total, age and geographical situation, all influence demand. Figure 1.6 shows the UK's ageing population: the number aged 65 or over increased by a quarter (to 9.3 million) between 1971 and 1997, leading to increased demand for firms supplying health care and other goods used by this sector. The number of under-16s has fallen, again affecting firms' levels of demand (e.g. for baby clothes). Changes in society also affect demand: an increase in the number of smaller family (e.g. lone parent) units encourages construction firms to make smaller properties, and changes in the number of couples both working affect the demand for convenience and 'fast' foods. Figure 1.7 highlights the growth of smaller-size households in the UK.

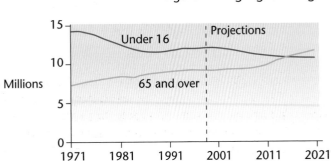

Figure 1.6 *UK population.* *Source: ONS 1999*

Size of household	1961 (%)	1994–5 (%)
1 person	14	27
2 people	30	34
3 people	23	16
4 or more people	33	23
Average size	3.1	2.4

Source: OPCS, 1996

Figure 1.7 *Household size, 1961 and 1994–5*

Markets and supply

AQA	M1, M3
EDEXCEL	M1
OCR	M1
WJEC	M1
NICCEA	M3

The fundamental law of supply is:

price ↑ = quantity supplied ↑; price ↓ = quantity supplied ↓

> The market supply curve shows that, at a price of £10, firms are prepared to supply 30,000 items.

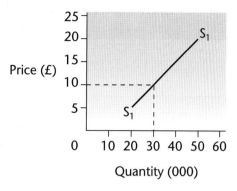

Figure 1.8 The supply curve

The higher the price, the higher the quantity supplied since higher prices lead to higher profits. Existing firms expand output and/or new firms enter the market.

Shifts in the supply curve

Movements along an existing supply curve – expansions or contractions of quantity supplied – occur when the price of the good or service changes. The supply curve itself can also move – a **shift in supply** – due to non-price factors.

Shifts in the supply curve result from:

> Technological developments are a good illustration, where cost-saving new machinery and automated processes improve productivity, reducing unit costs and increasing output.

Factor inputs

Changes in the price or ratio of individual factors of production a firm uses, or their quality, cause a change in the firm's production costs, which will affect supply levels.

> A change from S₁ to S₂ (Figure 1.9) shows that at a price of £10, firms will supply 35,000 items; a fall from S₁ to S₃ (Figure 1.10) means that firms will only supply 25,000 items.

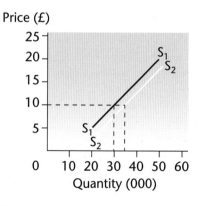

Figure 1.9 Increase in supply

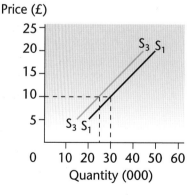

Figure 1.10 Decrease in supply

Other influences

Competition means increased efficiency in using resources, leading to higher output. With **jointly supplied goods**, such as petrol and other oils, an increase in the price of one good will increase not only its supply, but that of those jointly supplied with it. **Natural factors** can affect supply: e.g. global warming will affect crop and other agricultural production. **Government involvement**, e.g. through taxation, anti-pollution and anti-congestion policies, affects a firm's production costs and therefore its supply.

Changes in supply are different from change in quantity supplied.

Market and price

AQA	M1, M3
EDEXCEL	M1
OCR	M2, M3
WJEC	M1
NICCEA	M3

Prices can move freely. For example, if the price rose to £15:

- consumers demand 20,000
- but producers supply 40,000
- thus creating a surplus
- causing the price to fall
- which increases quantity demanded
- and reduces quantity supplied
- and so equilibrium is re-established.

If the demand and supply curves (Figs 1.3 and 1.8) are combined, the equilibrium market price is £10: consumers demand, and producers supply, 30,000 items.

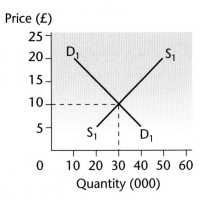

Figure 1.11 Equilibrium

The market, or equilibrium, price is established when demand equals supply.

Elasticity of demand

AQA	M1
EDEXCEL	M1
OCR	M2, M3
WJEC	M1
NICCEA	M3

The measure of a change in quantity demanded (or supplied) as a result of some external factor is known as **elasticity**. Elasticity of demand is affected by either:

the change in **price**   *or*   the change in **income**   *or*   the change in **prices of other goods**

Price elasticity of demand (PED)

The price elasticity of demand measures the responsiveness of the quantity demanded to a change in its price: we are examining **movements along the demand curve**, not changes in demand.

Price elasticity = $\dfrac{\text{Percentage change in quantity demanded}}{\text{Percentage change in price}}$

If, for example, price rises from £20 to £30 and quantity demanded falls from 400 to 300, PED = 25/50 = 0.5. If PED is below 1, as in this case, demand is known as **price-inelastic**. When PED is greater than 1, the supplier knows that a change in price will cause a more than proportionate change in quantity demanded: the product is price-sensitive, and demand is **price-elastic**. Where PED = 1, this is known as **unitary elasticity**: any given percentage price change results in the same percentage change in quantity demanded.

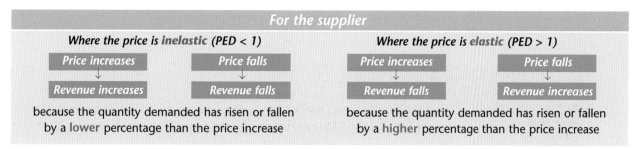

For the supplier

Where the price is inelastic (PED < 1)		*Where the price is elastic (PED > 1)*	
Price increases	Price falls	Price increases	Price falls
↓	↓	↓	↓
Revenue increases	Revenue falls	Revenue falls	Revenue increases
because the quantity demanded has risen or fallen by a **lower** percentage than the price increase		because the quantity demanded has risen or fallen by a **higher** percentage than the price increase	

Figure 1.12 Price elasticity and the supplier

Price elasticity is influenced by:

Availability of substitutes

Where a product has a close substitute, for example margarine and butter, demand tends to be elastic since it is easy for the user to switch between the substitutes. Where close substitutes do not exist, there is less competition and demand is more inelastic.

Percentage of spending on the product

Inexpensive products often have inelastic demands, because increases in price have little effect on consumers' spending plans. With higher-priced products, consumers search harder for alternatives or substitutes.

Addiction

Where consumers are stopped from making price-rational decisions, e.g. through alcohol or other drug addiction, price movements usually have little effect and price is inelastic.

Income elasticity of demand (IED)

Demand is **income-elastic** when IED is greater than 1, and **income-inelastic** when IED is less than 1.

IED measures **how demand responds to changes in consumer incomes.** IED can also be linked with shifts in the demand curve: page 22 identified changes in disposable income as an influence causing the curve to shift.

> Income elasticity = Percentage change in quantity demanded / Percentage change in income
>
> **KEY POINT**

Cross-elasticity of demand (CED)

CED measures how the demand for a good responds to changes in the price of a related (complementary or substitute) good, and is associated with shifts in the demand curve. The closer the complement or substitute, the higher the cross-elasticity: we would, for example, expect a higher cross-elasticity for different brands of jam than for the more distant substitutes of jam and cheese spread.

> Cross-elasticity = Percentage change in Product A's demand / Percentage change in Product B's price
>
> **KEY POINT**

Progress check

1 What effect might a cut in direct taxes have on demand levels?

2 Why is a price cut unlikely to benefit a firm with price-inelastic products?

2 Demand is not responsive to price changes. The lower price is not compensated for by increased sales, with an overall fall in revenue.

1 It will increase real disposable incomes and purchasing power, increasing overall demand. If supply cannot respond, there will be price increases.

1.4 International trade

After studying this section you should be able to:

- *compare and contrast free trade and protectionism*
- *assess the relevance of EU membership to UK firms*
- *explain the issues associated with floating and fixed exchange rates*

LEARNING SUMMARY

Specialisation and exchange

AQA	M3
EDEXCEL	M1
OCR	M1
WJEC	M1
NICCEA	M3

The UK was, and still is, noted for specialising in (e.g.) manufactured products and financial services.

Just as people specialise (i.e. division of labour), so do countries. Influences on specialisation include land and climate, availability of raw materials, and the level or training and expertise of the workforce. Specialist firms create mass production, producing surpluses to trade with other countries. Interdependence between trading countries exists, since specialisation means a country's resources are not being used by firms to make the other goods it needs.

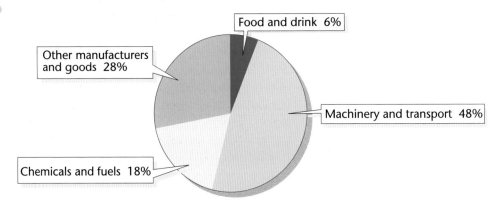

Figure 1.13 UK export of goods, by category, 1998
Source, ONS, 1999

Free trade

AQA	M3
EDEXCEL	M1
OCR	M1
WJEC	M1
NICCEA	M3

Free trade occurs when the movement of goods and services between countries is not restricted in any way. Firms benefit from specialisation and free trade through economies of scale leading to productive efficiency. Also, since countries cannot produce certain items efficiently (e.g. tropical foodstuffs in the UK's climate), trade leads to a greater choice of products being available for consumers.

Protectionism

Countries may restrict free trade from taking place. The government of a country uses protectionism for one or more purposes:

Purpose	Possible approach
to improve the country's balance of payments by reducing imports;	**quotas** – physical limits placed on amounts allowed into the country
to protect the exchange rate (page 29);	**exchange controls** – limit on the amount of foreign currency bought by firms/individuals
to raise revenue;	**tariffs** – taxes on imports making them more expensive than home-based goods
to safeguard domestic employment and 'infant industries' not yet strong enough to compete with imported competitor products	**subsidies** – financial support to industries to improve their competitive position

The VERA (Voluntary Export Restriction Agreement) between the UK and Japan has limited the import of Japanese cars into the UK.

The EU's **Common External Tariff** is applied to goods or services entering the EU: this encourages member states to import from other members due to the relative price benefit.

A government may also need to protect against the 'dumping' of goods from overseas competitors who are exporting at low prices to establish market penetration. It also has available the other protectionist methods of **embargoes** (refusing to trade in certain items for political or military reasons) or **procurement policies** (to 'buy from within').

Protectionism affects the benefits of free trade: there is less choice, consumers face higher prices, and inefficiency can result from reduced competition. There is also a danger that, if one country adopts protectionist measures, other countries will follow, thereby reducing overall world trade.

The European Union and other groupings

AQA	M3
EDEXCEL	M1
OCR	M1
WJEC	M1
NICCEA	A2

Free trade areas exist. NAFTA, the North American Free Trade Agreement, when formed in 1994, created the world's largest free trade zone with a population of nearly 400 million, and a combined gross national product of almost £5 billion (1998). **Supplier organisations** also exist: these are often producer countries wishing to exploit their dominance in a particular world market, e.g. OPEC (Organisation of Petroleum Exporting Countries), established in 1960 to gain some control over oil supply and prices.

The UK, France, Germany and Italy from the EU, together with the USA, Japan and Canada, make up the G7 group of industrialised countries. Russia, when included with these, forms the G8.

The European Union (EU) is an example of a **customs union**, with common institutions and common policies on trade, both between members and with the outside world. Although the USA and Japan are the world's two largest single industrialised economies, the EU as a whole is larger than either. It contains four of the **G7** group of industrialised economies, and seven of the world's 12 largest industrial economies are EU members. The UK is one of the poorest countries (measured by GDP per head), in 1999 ahead of only Greece, Portugal and Spain, even though Figure 1.14 shows it to be a net contributor to the EU budget.

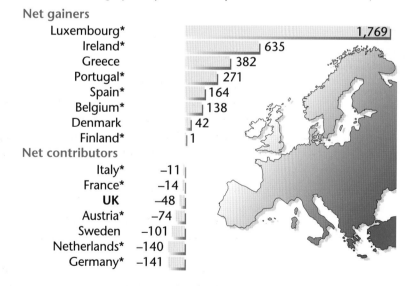

Average per capita net receipts/contributions – 1995–7, euros

Net gainers
- Luxembourg* — 1,769
- Ireland* — 635
- Greece — 382
- Portugal* — 271
- Spain* — 164
- Belgium* — 138
- Denmark — 42
- Finland* — 1

Net contributors
- Italy* — –11
- France* — –14
- **UK** — –48
- Austria* — –74
- Sweden — –101
- Netherlands* — –140
- Germany* — –141

Figure 1.14 *EU membership (* indicates those countries adopting the Euro, 1999)*

The Single Market

Promoting trade between members was a major reason behind the formation of what is now the EU. The Single Market Act 1986 sought to: **remove** barriers to trade, controls on the flow of capital, and abuse of market power; and to **establish** free movement of labour and goods, and common technical and other standards. The Single Market is a major influence on UK businesses.

Common standards

EU-wide standards of quality and safety are set, and UK manufacturers must ensure their products meet these standards, for example as stated in Directives on food labelling and toy safety (see page 69).

Open markets

These now exist in areas such as information and communications technology, and financial services. UK firms face increased competition through these open markets with their common standards.

Free movement of labour and goods

Free movement of labour is a basic principle of the EU, and the increased recognition and standardisation of professional qualifications may improve the employment prospects for UK nationals and influence employment policies of UK firms. There are few cross-border formalities or delays in transporting goods throughout the Union.

Other EU activities

The **European Investment Bank** (EIB) grants loans: for example, UK firms received loans to construct the Channel Tunnel and to develop North Sea oil and gas fields. The EIB promotes European integration by regional development in economically disadvantaged areas, improving communications, and environmental protection. It also seeks to improve co-operation with non-member countries.

Supporting world trade

The role of the **International Monetary Fund** (IMF) is to encourage greater co-operation between countries in formulating economic policy. It was created following a worldwide economic depression in the 1930s, in an attempt to stop such an event happening again, and to avoid protectionism affecting international trade. It has nearly 200 member countries who agree to be open about how they determine their currency's value: the IMF monitors exchange policies.

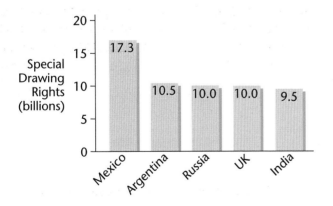

Figure 1.15 *Main users of IMF finance, 1947–97*
Source: IMF, 1998

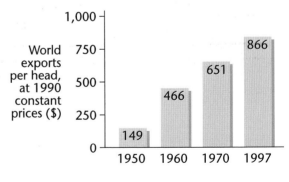

Figure 1.16 *Growth in world trade, 1950–97*

The WTO's 134 members launched the Millennium Round of trade negotiations in Seattle (USA), 1999.

The main function of the **World Trade Organisation** (WTO) is to help trade flow as freely as possible, e.g. by removing tariffs. It is also a forum for trade negotiations, and it handles trade disputes. The WTO developed from the General Agreement on Tariffs and Trade (GATT), but has a wider influence (whereas GATT dealt with goods only, the WTO includes services).

From the late 1940s to date, GATT and the WTO worked to liberalise trade, through a sets of talks, or **Rounds**: the most recent, the 'Uruguay Round', was held for over seven years and resulted in a 38 per cent reduction in tariffs.

Exchange rates

AQA	M3
EDEXCEL	M1
OCR	M1
WJEC	M1
NICCEA	M1

> **KEY POINT**
>
> The exchange rate of a currency is expressed as its value in other currencies. This is particularly important for importers and exporters, who could find that their profit margins are affected by the change in the relative prices of the different currencies they are using in international trade.

Under a **floating exchange rate** system, the rate (price) is determined by market forces, i.e. the demand for and supply of the currency on the foreign exchange market. A government will sell or buy some of its reserves of foreign currency to influence the exchange rate and even-out major fluctuations. It may also alter domestic interest rates to control short-term speculative capital movements.

A floating exchange rate should solve balance of payments problems. If the UK becomes less competitive internationally:

it suffers a deficit in its balance of payments	increased imports will increase the supply of, and lower exports will reduce the demand for sterling,	so the value of sterling will fall, raising import prices and reducing export prices	which leads back to equilibrium.

However, floating exchange rates encourage **speculation**: speculators gamble on future changes in these rates, their actions affecting the rate which is the focus for speculation. A **fixed rate** system is the alternative, and has often been tried (e.g. the EU's **Exchange Rate Mechanism (ERM)**). Under this system, governments agree the rate at which their currencies are fixed and exchanged, within set limits.

> **KEY POINT**
>
> The advantage to firms trading in overseas markets is that a fixed exchange rate brings greater certainty that profit margins will be maintained.

In the ERM, the UK had an exchange rate of 2.95 Deutschmarks to the pound (within an agreed margin).

When the UK was a member of the ERM, the value of the pound 'floated' against other currencies. Sterling was forced out of the ERM in September 1992 by speculative pressures on the currency, and on leaving the ERM the pound was allowed to float and to find its own value.

Progress check

1 Identify **three** effects on a UK firm resulting from the increased mobility of labour within the European Union.

2 If a government introduces tariffs on a range of imported goods, why might demand for these goods remain at the same level?

2 The goods may be necessities rather than luxuries (e.g. certain foodstuffs), or vital fuel or raw materials (e.g. coal, iron ore) not found in the home country, or unique (e.g. certain medical drugs). Without substitutes being available, their inelastic demand will lead to imports continuing.

1 (a) Increased competition in the labour market, leading to quicker labour turnover;
(b) increased labour turnover leads to higher costs of recruitment, selection and training (e.g. induction training);
(c) a much wider range of candidates, from across the EU.

Sample questions and model answers

1

Why are exclusively 'market' and 'planned' economies not found in practice?   [20]

> There are several reasons why countries have mixed economies. These include:
> - The socially undesirable results of a market economy need to be regulated by the state.
> - In a pure market economy, income distribution is not affected by non-economic factors. In practice, the state has to make decisions on how taxation and other influences on income will affect the distribution of this income.
> - The state also needs to ensure a suitable balance between social factors and the influence of profit. For example, in the 1990s the fatal accidents that occurred on the UK's railway network reopened the debate about the balance between profit and safety levels.

Examples include the control of private monopolies, consumer protection law, and health and safety legislation.

Examples include the trend for UK governments to move from direct to indirect taxes, and the debate on tax harmonisation in the European Union.

2

(a) What factors affect how the demand for a firm's product reacts to a change in its price or in the price of another item?   [5]

(b) If VAT was added on books, how would this affect their demand?   [5]

> (a) Factors influencing the demand include: what proportion of disposable income is spent on the product; whether there is a substitute product available; whether the product is a luxury item or a necessity (affecting its price elasticity of demand); and whether the product is in some way connected to the other item (e.g. complementary demand).
>
> (b) VAT on books would cause the price of the books to rise, affecting the level of demand, which would almost certainly fall. The supply of the books is likely to remain fairly constant, since the increase in price due to VAT will not greatly affect manufacturers' profits. Demand falling, against constant supply, will lead to a new equilibrium position. The situation is complicated by a number of factors, such as the elasticity of demand: for example, if the books are textbooks there may be substitute sources of information, such as the Internet available, or if they are for leisure reading the demand on library services may rise as a result.

Use examples, such as those in this study guide (page 22) to illustrate your points.

You can comment on the different forms of elasticity when answering this question.

Practice examination questions

1 A manufacturer discovers that the demand for its well-known chocolate bar varies with price as shown in the schedule below:

Price in pence	Quantity demanded in million bars per year
35	50
34	52
33	54
32	56
31	58
30	60
29	62
28	64
27	66
26	68
25	70

(a) Calculate and comment upon the price-elasticity of demand when price rises from 30p to 32p. [2]

(b) Assess the possible effects on the firm of a rise in the price of a product which is a close substitute and evaluate the responses which the firm might make. [9]

(c) Assess the possible effects on the firm of a sharp rise in consumers' disposable income. [6]

(d) Analyse the effects of a vigorous 'healthy eating' campaign by the government upon this firm and evaluate possible responses the firm might make. [11]

Edexcel Specimen Paper, Unit 1

2 Study the following information and then answer the questions that follow.

This diagram summarises a sporting event's supply of tickets and the demand for them. There is a maximum price set for tickets.

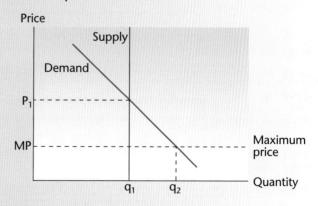

(a) Why is the supply curve drawn as shown above? [3]

(b) Why does setting a maximum price encourage the development of a black market? [3]

(c) How might the tickets be allocated? [6]

(d) Why do governments choose to interfere in markets? Give **two** examples. [6]

Chapter 2

Business organisations

The following topics are covered in this chapter:

- *Structure of the UK economy*
- *Main features of the private sector*
- *Organisations in the private sector*

- *The public sector*
- *Stakeholders*

2.1 Structure of the UK economy

After studying this section you should be able to:

- *describe briefly the two sectors of the UK's mixed economy*
- *name the main types of organisation in both sectors*

LEARNING SUMMARY

The private and public sectors

AQA	M2, M3
EDEXCEL	M1
OCR	M1
WJEC	M1
NICCEA	M1

Businesses in the UK are normally grouped into private sector and public sector organisations. **Private sector** firms are set up by individuals, **entrepreneurs** who seek to make profit from their business activities. Although many private sector firms are **controlled** by entrepreneur(s), they may be **owned** by different people (or organisations), for example, companies owned by **shareholders**, either as private or institutional (organisation-based) investors. This may lead to a conflict between ownership and control (see page 38).

As well as making profit, entrepreneurs may have other objectives, e.g.:

- job satisfaction
- employment
- power and prestige.

The **public sector** consists of those organisations owned and/or financed by central and local government. This sector provides goods and services to the community through public corporations, local government and other statutory agencies (e.g. the National Health Service). The profit motive is not so prominent: the emphasis in the public sector is on providing for the community by the community, using funding supplied through taxes and government borrowing.

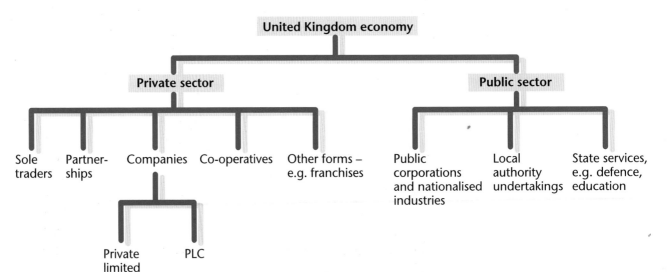

Figure 2.1 *Types of organisations in the UK economy*

2.2 Main features of the private sector

After studying this section you should be able to:

- *explain the importance of profit to an entrepreneur*
- *describe the relevance of incorporation and limited liability to business*
- *explain the nature and purpose of mission statements and corporate objectives*

Entrepreneurs and profit

AQA	M3
EDEXCEL	M1
OCR	M1
WJEC	M1
CCEA	M1

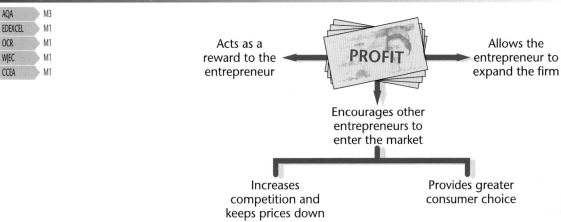

Acts as a reward to the entrepreneur ← **PROFIT** → **Allows the entrepreneur to expand the firm**

↓ **Encourages other entrepreneurs to enter the market**

Increases competition and keeps prices down | **Provides greater consumer choice**

Figure 2.2 Profit

Why is profit important to an entrepreneur? It provides **a measure of success** for the business, as well as acting as an **indicator** to others. Prospective lenders use the profit figure to decide whether to lend, and potential entrepreneurs look at present profit levels when deciding whether to enter the industry.

> Economists view **profit** as the reward of one of the factors of production (**enterprise**).

Profit, as the reward for taking risk, is not guaranteed: many firms make losses and close. Even when profit is made, it may be small and regarded by the entrepreneur as poor reward for risk-taking: the firm's **profitability** is too low. This results in continual change in the structure of the private sector.

> The Department of Trade and Industry regards its estimates of firms registering and de-registering for VAT as the best official guide to business start-ups and closures.

Year	Registrations		De-registrations	
	(000)	**Rate**	**(000)**	**Rate**
1994	168.2	36	188.1	40
1995	164.0	35	173.2	37
1996	168.2	36	165.1	35
1997	182.6	39	164.5	35
1998	186.3	40	155.9	33

Figure 2.3 VAT registrations and de-registrations, 1994–98: UK, thousands and rate per 10,000 resident adults   Source: DTI SME (Small and Medium Enterprise) Statistics Unit

Industry	Registrations (000)	De-registrations (000)
Agriculture, fishing, mining, energy	4.1	6.0
Manufacturing	12.6	14.9
Construction	18.4	17.4
Hotels, catering	16.8	16.3
Transport	9.3	8.2
Finance and business services	68.7	36.0

Figure 2.4 Enterprises registering and de-registering by industry, 1998 (000)
Source: DTI SME Statistics Unit

Figure 2.3 shows that there were 186,300 registrations in the UK in 1998, and 155,900 de-registrations (1 in 9 of the businesses registered at the start of the year). The number registered in 1998 had risen by 2% on 1997, to its highest level for five years. Figure 2.4 illustrates the move from the primary and secondary sectors to the tertiary sector (see page 19). In 1998, the number of registrations fell compared with 1997 in agriculture/fishing (600) and manufacturing (900): in the same period, de-registrations for agriculture/fishing and manufacturing both rose by 100. The net result was a loss of some 4,000 businesses, compared with a net gain of nearly 33,000 in business services: this industry grew by over 100,000 in the five years to 1998, to 1 in 4 of all VAT registered UK businesses.

UK, number

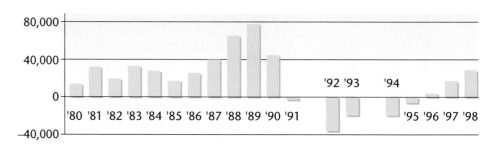

Figure 2.5 *Net change in VAT registered enterprises, 1980–98*
Source: DTI SME Statistics Unit

> Individuals in the private sector try to make profit by acting as entrepreneurs in the market-place. The profit motive forms the foundation of the private sector.
>
> **KEY POINT**

Legal liability and legal status

AQA	M3
EDEXCEL	M1
OCR	M1
WJEC	M1
NICCEA	M1

Other companies, for example some examination bodies and professional associations, are **limited by guarantee**; members of such a company guarantee its business debts, up to a given maximum.

A limited company has the legal authority to:
- own property
- enter contracts in its own name
- sue (and be sued) in the courts.

Most large commercial companies are **limited by share** and must include 'limited' or 'plc' as appropriate in their name. This acts as a warning to those trading with such a company because any debts it incurs from trading may not be recoverable due to the **limited liability** of its owners (shareholders).

Where a limited company cannot pay its debts from its own financial resources, it cannot make the owners use their personal finances to meet these debts. Sole traders and partnerships have **unlimited liability**: if business debts cannot be met from the firm's own resources, the owner(s) can be forced to sell personal assets to cover these business debts.

Limited liability encourages greater investment than would otherwise take place, and ensures a demand for stocks and shares.

> The benefit of limited liability to the economy is that it encourages people to risk owning and/or investing in companies, because they know their liability (losses) will be limited to the amount they have agreed to invest.
>
> **KEY POINT**

Another important difference between these forms of business ownership is in their **legal status**. Limited companies are **incorporated bodies**. 'Incorporation' means that a company has a **separate legal existence** from its members (shareholders). Sole traders and partnerships are **unincorporated** businesses and do not have a legal existence that is separate from that of the owners.

Goals and objectives

AQA	M3
EDEXCEL	M1
OCR	M1
WJEC	M1
NICCEA	M1

Our reason for being

To dedicate our business to the pursuit of social and environmental change.

To creatively balance the financial and human needs of our stakeholders: employees, franchisees, customers, suppliers and shareholders.

To courageously ensure that our business is ecologically sustainable: meeting the needs of the present without compromising the future.

To meaningfully contribute to local, national and international communities in which we trade, by adopting a code of conduct which ensures care, honesty, fairness and respect.

To passionately campaign for the protection of the environment, human and civil rights, and against animal testing within the cosmetics and toiletries industry.

To tirelessly work to narrow the gap between principles and practice, whilst making fun, passion and care part of our daily lives.

Mission statement, The Body Shop International plc, 1999

Firms set themselves goals to achieve. The **mission statement** of a company states its overall aim and purpose. This is then translated into **corporate objectives**.

Corporate objective	Value to the firm
Increase market share and become the market leader	*Greater control over market price, easier to get new products accepted*
Maximise profits	*Pleases shareholders and improves share price*
Ensure long-term growth and stability	*Economies of scale; helps protect the company from being taken over*
Stay a market leader through technological innovation	*Remain competitive in the market*
Diversify in order to develop new markets	*Exploit profitable markets; spread the risk by operating in different markets*

> **KEY POINT**
>
> Corporate objectives become measurable when developed into more detailed **functional** objectives: these are expanded into **individual** objectives for employees to achieve. Achievement can be measured through **appraisal** of individuals and by adopting a **management by objectives** (MBO) approach.

Progress check

1 State **two** reasons why profit is important to an entrepreneur.

2 What is the main difference between an incorporated and an unincorporated business?

2 An incorporated business has a separate legal existence. An unincorporated business has no separate legal existence, and therefore legal actions must be taken (or defended) personally by the owner(s).

1 It acts as income, i.e. the reward for enterprise; it is also a measure of success.

2.3 Organisations in the private sector

After studying this section you should be able to:

- evaluate sole traders and partnerships as forms of business ownership
- compare and contrast limited companies with unincorporated businesses
- analyse 'the divorce of ownership and control'
- outline the business nature of (a) franchises; (b) co-operatives; (c) 'mutuality' in the UK economy

LEARNING SUMMARY

Sole traders and partnerships

AQA	M3
EDEXCEL	M1
OCR	M1
WJEC	M1
NICCEA	M1

A **sole trader** (proprietor) business exists when, even though there may be a number of employees, there is only **one owner**.

The sole trader form of business ownership tends to occur where:

- personal services are provided
- little capital is needed to start up business
- large-scale production is not a feature.

are often small, and any losses are borne by the sole trader	**PROFITS**	do not have to be shared with others
capital is not easy to obtain and cannot be obtained from a share issue	**SETTING UP**	little capital is needed, and there are few formalities
the burden is not shared with others; typically long hours and little chance of holidays	**CONTROL**	easy to keep overall control, and be 'your own boss'
might have to be made without assistance	**DECISIONS**	can be made quickly

Figure 2.6 *Features of the sole trader*

Partnerships are also unincorporated businesses with unlimited liability. They are traditionally associated with professions such as accountants and lawyers, where capital outlay is small. The minimum number of partners is two and the maximum is (normally) 20. Partners often draw up a written agreement expressing the rights and duties of individual partners with reference to:

- profit-sharing
- amounts of capital to be contributed
- the different business responsibilities of each partner
- regulations concerning the withdrawal of profits by individual partners
- regulations on introducing new partners and the dissolution (ending) of the partnership.

The rules laid down in the Partnership Act 1890 apply where there is no agreement.

- Profits and losses are shared equally.
- Partners' loans receive 5% interest per annum.
- Each partner has an equal say in how the partnership operates.

A partnership, like a sole trader business, is **simple to establish**. Other similarities are that the partnership can also **keep its financial affairs private**, and that the owners still face the drawback of **unlimited liability**. If a sole trader is thinking of converting to a partnership, the key issues to consider are:

Benefits	Drawbacks
specialisation can take place (each partner can specialise in a different business function)	**decision-making may take longer** (the new partner must be consulted)
additional skills may also be introduced by the new partner	if/when the new partner dies or leaves, a **new partnership** must be created
more capital is available (an extra owner is an extra investor)	the **profit must be shared** between the partners
expansion is therefore easier	**control** of the business must also be shared

Limited companies

AQA — M3
EDEXCEL — M1
OCR — M1
WJEC — M1
NICCEA — M1

Incorporation gives a limited company a **separate legal existence** from its owners (shareholders). There are over 1 million limited companies registered in the UK, varying in size from small family-owned businesses to large PLCs.

Private and public companies

A limited company is classed as **private** (Ltd) unless its memorandum of association states that it is a **public limited company** (PLC). A private company cannot advertise its shares for sale to the public or through the Stock Exchange: its share capital must not exceed £50,000.

PLCs must have a minimum £50,000 share capital, and can sell their shares to the public and may be quoted on the Stock Exchange. A **Stock Exchange** acts as the market for second-hand stocks and shares (securities). It therefore encourages investment in business, offering investors a degree of protection through its strict rules for admitting firms. The **Alternative Investment Market** (AIM) exists for companies that are too small (or young) to be quoted on the London Stock Exchange.

The Stock Exchange in London is one of the largest in the world.

In 1999, changes were made to how the London Stock Exchange classifies shares. These changes reflected the increasing importance of 'information technology' companies, anticipated the expected effects of Europe's single currency, and helped investors to invest in shares less affected by economic recession (by dividing stock into 'cyclical' and 'non-cyclical' categories).

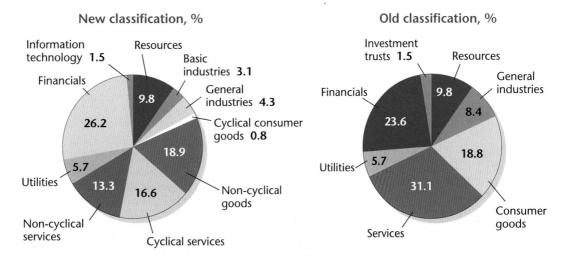

Figure 2.7 *The 'new look' FTSE index*

> PLCs find it easier to raise finance, tend to be much larger than private companies, and find ownership and control more clearly separated.
>
> **KEY POINT**

The comparison with sole traders and partnerships

- Limited liability is offered to investors, encouraging greater investment.
- Greater investment = greater size = greater economies of scale.
- Through its separate legal existence from the owners, the company owns assets, takes legal action in its own name, and does not face problems of continuity when an owner dies, retires or otherwise leaves.

  but
- Greater expense and more formalities are incurred in setting up the company.
- Its business affairs are less private.
- Greater size may result in diseconomies of scale.
- Owners of private companies may face difficulties in selling shares.
- Ownership of PLCs can be transferred (via the Stock Exchange) against the wishes of the directors, and shareholders may seek to operate short-term policies to make short-term profits, all leading to greater instability.

Registering a company

The Companies Act 1985 sets out the legal requirements to create and run a company. All companies are registered at the Companies Registration Office. Limited companies must submit annual returns summarising changes to their affairs, and annual financial statements, including the directors' report, profit and loss account and balance sheet, and the auditors' report.

The Memorandum of Association governs the relationship of the company with the outside world. Its clauses include:

Name	The proposed company name
Situation	The address of the registered office
Objects	The purposes for which it was formed (stated in general terms)
Liability	A statement that its members have limited liability
Capital	The amount of capital registered and the types of shares
Association	Directors' names and addresses

The Articles of Association govern the internal workings of the company, including details of directors (number, rights and duties), the conduct and calling of meetings, and the division of profits.

'Divorce of ownership and control'

This phrase is closely associated with PLCs: shareholders own the company but do not control it. Few shareholders have a direct say in the daily running of the PLC, because – through the Annual General Meeting (AGM) – they appoint specialist directors to exercise effective day-to-day control on their behalf.

Once ownership and control is separated in this way, the decisions made by the directors – the controllers – may clash with the wishes of (some of) the shareholders – the owners. A common example is where the shareholders may wish to see a policy of profit maximisation, which may not be the wish of directors who see long-term growth as a more important strategy to pursue.

Progress check

1 Name **three** occupations where sole traders are commonly found.
2 State **two** reasons why sole traders may choose to convert their businesses into limited companies rather than partnerships.

2 To gain limited liability; easier to obtain more capital.

1 Hairdressers; plumbers; builders.

Other forms of ownership

AQA	M3
EDEXCEL	M1
OCR	M1
WJEC	M1
NICCEA	M1

Some 70% of McDonald's 26,500 outlets world-wide are franchised (1999).

Franchises

These businesses use the name and logo of an existing company. Franchising is a major growth area in the UK economy: by the end of 1999 there were nearly 600 business format franchises in the UK, comprising almost 30,000 franchisees who employed nearly a quarter of a million people. Examples include **The Body Shop**, which opened its first franchise in 1977, **Thornton's Confectionery**, **Prontaprint Ltd** and **ANC** package delivery service.

> Franchisees need the use of a car, a telephone, a reasonable size room at home (or use of the garage), plus plenty of energy and determination. **Card Connection** will provide everything else needed to make the business a success.
>
> *Source: Card Connection, 1999*

> Our commitment to franchising derives from sound business reasons. Fundamental to our long term success story has been the innovative ideas and contribution of our franchisees. Without them, **McDonald's** would not be what it is today.
>
> *Source: McDonald's, 1999*

The franchisee buys the franchise, entering into a contract with and paying a fee to the franchisor (the company). Typically:

The franchisee:
- agrees to follow set rules, e.g. layout of premises and product standards
- buys only from the franchisor or other named supplier

The franchisor:
- supplies the decor and assists with layout
- allows the franchisee to use the product and the logo

Types of franchise agreements include:
- manufacturer–retailer (some petrol stations and car dealers)
- wholesaler–retailer (Spar and other voluntary groups)
- trademark–retailer ('fast food' outlets).

- The franchisor can expand without making a large capital investment, since the franchisee provides the capital. The company knows that its franchisees, who are not on a salary, will be highly motivated by the direct financial incentive to make their franchise a financial success.
- The franchisee gains a recognised product or service backed by successful marketing and business methods, and receives expert business support: success is therefore more likely than for an 'independent' entrepreneur.

The **British Franchise Association** (BFA) regulates franchising in the UK. The BFA is a non-profitmaking body, promoting ethical franchising through its member franchisor companies.

> The franchisee agreement grants the right and authorisation to operate a specific McDonald's restaurant, usually for a period of 20 years. These rights include the use of McDonald's trademarks, restaurant decor designs, signage and equipment layout, the formula and specifications for menu items, use of McDonald's method of operation, inventory control, book-keeping, accounting and marketing and the right to occupy the restaurant premises.
>
> In return, the franchisee agrees to operate the business in accordance with McDonald's standards of quality, service, cleanliness and value. The franchisee is expected to become involved in their community's civic and charitable activities. Training is a top priority to ensure the uniformity of the operation and the consistent quality of staff.
>
> Each franchisee has constant support through their own McDonald's consultant who is always available for help and advice, visiting the restaurant on a regular basis. Training facilities are free and available to the franchisee and their management team.
>
> *Extract from franchise agreement, McDonald's*

This extract is a clear indication of how a franchisor–franchisee relationship can operate.

Co-operatives

Although the larger UK co-operatives operate as limited companies, owning capital is not the dominating factor in the co-operative movement. Most co-operative societies exist to provide a service for their member-owners and for the public. Control is shared democratically, with each member having a single vote: trading surpluses ('profits') are often distributed to the members in proportion to their trade with the society.

Consumer co-operatives, where customers collectively own the business, are found in Europe and Japan: types of these in the UK include housing co-operatives and credit unions (formed to allow people to benefit from collective saving and borrowing). There are over 4,000 local co-operative **retail** societies (CRS) – the 'Co-ops' – in the UK. Many of their products come from the **Co-operative Wholesale Society Ltd** (CWS): its role is to buy in bulk and to supply the retail co-ops with its own (about 3,000 own-brand) goods. The CWS is also the UK's largest farmer. Other co-operative activities include banking and insurance.

Producer (worker) co-operatives also exist. There are over 1,000 worker co-operatives, many of them having existed previously in a different ownership form: printing/publishing, fashion/textiles and agriculture are popular areas. **ICOM**, the federation of worker co-operatives, was formed in 1971 and supports its members by providing training and business advice: local **Co-operative Development Agencies** also support these worker co-operatives.

The **Co-operative Retail Trading Group** (CRTG) links individual retail co-operatives. By 1999 the CRTG accounted for over 90% of co-operative food buying power.

Mutuality

Some building societies and life assurance firms are non-profitmaking organisations, existing for the benefit of their members (customers). In the 1990s, many changed status (e.g. the Halifax converted from a building society to a bank, becoming a limited company), producing cash 'windfalls' for the existing members, many of whom became shareholders.

> Many commentators argue that the new profit-focused companies now operate in the interests of their new owners (shareholders), having to meet new priorities such as profitability and dividend payment: this can be at the expense of the old priorities based on satisfying the old owners (customers).

KEY POINT

Progress check

1 Identify **two** differences between a franchisee and a sole trader.

2 What forms of co-operative exist in the UK?

2 Consumer (retail) co-operatives; producer (worker) co-operatives.

1 Franchisee operates within framework set by franchisor – sole trader is independent. Franchisee pays royalty to franchisor – sole trader keeps all net profit (after tax).

2.4 The public sector

After studying this section you should be able to:

LEARNING SUMMARY

- describe the nature, operation and control of a public corporation
- compare and contrast the benefits and drawbacks associated with (a) nationalisation and (b) privatisation

Public corporations, nationalisation and privatisation

AQA	M3
EDEXCEL	M1
OCR	M1
WJEC	M1
NICCEA	M1

A July 1999 White Paper gave the Post Office greater commercial freedom to do business, operating as a PLC whilst remaining in the public sector (the government owning all the shares). The White Paper proposed to cut its monopoly on letters from items costing £1 or less to items costing 50p or less; in return, the Post Office will be able to keep far more of its profits to invest in improved services.

Public corporations have a **separate legal existence** through the Act of Parliament creating them. Their assets are owned by the state on behalf of the community. Their objectives, whilst influenced by commercial considerations, often emphasise **social aspects**. They normally have **financial targets** to achieve, such as a target return on capital employed. A public corporation is controlled:

- by its government minister and through a board appointed by the minister;
- by a consumer council protecting the consumer interest;
- through being audited by the Competition Commission.

Nationalisation takes an industry into public ownership. Industries such as coal, gas and the railways were nationalised following the Second World War. By the end of the 1970s, however, many nationalised industries were regarded as inefficient and over-subsidised **monopolies**, lacking competition and being in a position to exploit their monopoly status. The government's response was to **privatise** – return to private ownership – most nationalised industries.

> A criticism of recently privatised industries is that their monopoly power may still remain. These 'privatised monopolies' are therefore regulated by 'watchdogs', e.g. OFGAS (gas), OFTEL (telephones) and OFWAT (water).
>
> KEY POINT

Recent privatisation in the UK includes:

- 1979 BP
- 1981 British Sugar
- 1983 Forestry Commission
- 1984 Sealink
- 1988 British Steel, Rover
- 1990/91 Electricity (supply and generation)

Other criticisms include:

- Privatising 'natural monopoly' industries may mean losing economies of scale.
- Private monopolies are likely to be less well regulated than public sector ones.
- Revenue from state-owned assets has been used for government current expenditure rather than for long-term investment.

Deregulation has also been used by the UK government (and the EU) to stimulate competition. Examples include transport services, and broadcasting.

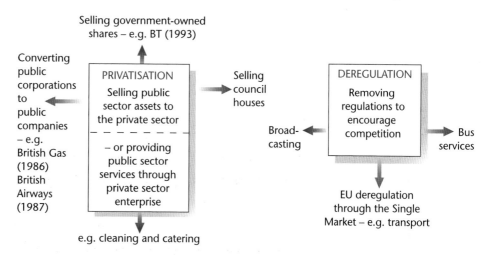

Figure 2.8 Privatisation and deregulation

2.5 Stakeholders

LEARNING SUMMARY

After studying this section you should be able to:

- *define the term 'stakeholder' and give relevant examples*
- *compare the shareholder concept with the stakeholder concept*

The nature of stakeholders

AQA	M3
EDEXCEL	M1
OCR	M1, M3
WJEC	M1
NICCEA	M1

Stakeholders are individuals or groups that have an influence on, or are influenced by, an organisation's decisions.

> Shell companies recognise five areas of responsibility:
>
> 1 To shareholders
> 2 To customers
> 3 To employees
> 4 To those with whom they do business
> 5 To society
>
> *Source: Royal Dutch/Shell Group of Companies, 1997*

Customers
Suppliers   Shareholders

THE FIRM
Directors
Managers
Employees

Local   Lenders
community

Figure 2.9 Internal and external stakeholders

The organisation's directors and managers face a possible conflict between their duty to stakeholders and their duty to shareholders. Because shareholders appoint directors and (through the directors) employ managers to run the firm, directors and managers should undertake policies for the benefit of the shareholders. This **shareholder concept** implies policies maximising share price and dividend should be followed at the expense of other policies.

The objectives of other stakeholder groups may conflict with this, and there may also be conflict between the objectives of any two stakeholder groups. For example, improving employee morale and efficiency by training will increase costs and affect profit (in the short term); by establishing closer links with a supplier, a company may start using new manufacturing processes that will affect its relationships with the local community. In the longer run there may not be a conflict: improvements for employees, better links with suppliers and customers improve quality, efficiency and profitability, and therefore bring higher profits.

Stakeholder and policy/action	Benefit
Close involvement with **local community**	*Good publicity for the firm; support from local community when needed*
Improving working conditions for **employees**	*Improved morale and motivation; higher profits; reduced labour turnover*
Better links with **suppliers** and **lenders**	*Good long-term relationships; better communication; better quality*

Progress check

1 Identify **three** differences between a public corporation and a PLC.
2 Give **two** disadvantages to a consumer when buying from a monopoly.

2 Little consumer choice; higher prices through lack of competition.

1 Corporations owned by the state; PLCs by shareholders; corporations controlled by minister/board, PLCs by Companies Acts; corporations' primary objective normally to serve general public, PLCs normally to optimise profit.

Sample questions and model answers

1

What difficulties does a sole trader face?   [10]

Try a structured approach, using key words/areas

Sole traders face these difficulties:

(a) **Financial.** Due to their relative lack of size, and the limited security they can offer lenders, sole traders often find it difficult to raise finance from lenders. This means opportunities for expansion are limited. In addition, the small size of most sole traders stops them benefiting from economies of scale. Cash flow problems are also experienced by many sole traders, due to their typical lack of power or market control.

(b) **Personal.** There is a substantial personal commitment required, in time and effort. There are limited opportunities for time off/holidays, and problems of continuity exist since the sole trader is an unincorporated business. Perhaps the greatest personal difficulty is that of unlimited liability.

You could include examples of sole traders to help explain your general points

(c) **Structural.** The single-owner nature of sole traders means that they are often non-specialists who lack expertise in many aspects of business life (although they can, of course, employ specialists). Although they can usually adapt quickly to changing market conditions, sole traders face difficulty competing with firms that have greater market control and resources (e.g. for advertising). The sole trader is often dependent on other, larger firms (e.g. for supply).

2

What are the arguments in favour of (a) nationalisation; (b) privatisation?   [10]

Try to present a balanced argument

Arguments for **nationalisation**:

(a) Natural monopolies (such as water) exist: their supply should be owned and controlled by the State for the benefit of all.

(b) Economic and defence considerations: some industries, such as fuel, are vital to the economy of the country.

(c) Regional and social arguments: relatively unprofitable (e.g. rural rail and postal) services may not otherwise be supplied; some firms were nationalised to avoid collapse and the creation of pockets of high unemployment.

With this topic, arguments in favour of the one approach are not necessarily arguments against the other. Look for specific points, e.g. 'raising revenue'.

(d) Cost considerations: the extent of capital investment required may rule out private sector interest due to risk and no guarantee of return on investment.

Arguments for **privatisation**:

(a) Raising revenue: a short-term one-off source of government income.

(b) Promoting competition: nationalisation creates inefficient monopolies.

(c) Reducing the Public Sector Borrowing Requirement (PSBR): a means of reducing government spending.

You may not receive marks if 'for' points in one part of your answer are repeated as 'against' points in the other part of your answer: this may amount to repetition.

(d) Political considerations: the move towards a 'popular capitalism' through greater share ownership, since the 1980s.

Practice examination questions

1 Examine the factors that the directors of a company must consider when deciding whether to change its legal status from that of a private limited company to that of a public limited company. [10]

2 (a) What is a 'franchise'? [2]

(b) Give **three** reasons why a person might take out a franchise. [6]

(c) Why might firms sell franchises instead of opening shops themselves? [4]

(d) To what extent does taking out a franchise affect the benefits of operating as an independent sole trader? [6]

3 "Why not get the private sector to provide all our education and health services?"

Examine the validity of this statement. [8]

4 The European Union's Common Agricultural Policy controls the production of crops and livestock.

Analyse the effects of controlling the rearing of pigs on the stakeholders in this industry. [8]

Chapter 3

Structure and growth

The following topics are covered in this chapter:

- Internal organisation
- Features of organisational structures
- Communication in the organisation
- Size and growth
- Economies of scale

3.1 Internal organisation

After studying this section you should be able to:

- describe line, line and staff, and matrix forms of organisational structure
- differentiate between role and task cultures

LEARNING SUMMARY

Forms of organisational structure

AQA	M2
EDEXCEL	M1
OCR	M2, M3
WJEC	M1
NICCEA	M2

A firm's management carries out a number of functions. These include:

- **planning**: an example is strategic planning to ensure the firm's future
- **controlling**: for example, implementing budgetary control
- **co-ordinating**: e.g. making sure there is efficient communication.

Management achieves these by operating within a suitable organisational structure. Nowadays it is recognised that there is no one best structure for all organisations: there are many influences that determine the best structure for an organisation, regardless of size, form of ownership or sector in which it is based.

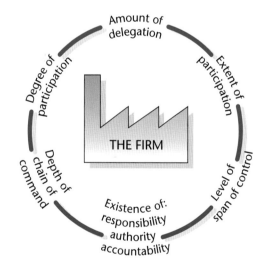

Figure 3.1 Influences on a firm's internal organisation

Line, and line and staff organisational structures

The best illustrations of functional organisations have often been private sector firms working in the secondary sector of industry.

Most UK organisations were traditionally organised internally on the basis of the different **business functions** such as controlling finance, making items, dealing with employees, selling to customers, and buying stock. The main departments – Personnel, Accounts, Production, Purchasing and Sales/Marketing – reflect these functions. This form of corporate culture is often called **role** culture because individual roles are clearly defined, for example by job descriptions.

The formal, traditional organisational system based on these functions is called **line organisation**. The advantage of this organisational structure is that roles and responsibilities are well-defined with a clear chain of command.

> **KEY POINT**
>
> A line structure tends to be bureaucratic in nature, with a narrow span of control due to the many layers of hierarchy.

> A good illustration is the frequent use of consultants by larger companies.

As they grow, firms rely more on specialist support functions and personnel. A **line and staff** organisation recognises the importance of these specialists.

> Organised into five core businesses ... Shell companies operate independently, although they draw on a common network of service companies ... The service companies provide a range of specialist advice and resources...
>
> Shell's Energy *(extract), Royal Dutch/Shell Group of Companies, 1999*

Problems can arise with line and staff structures:

- a lack of 'line' understanding of 'staff' procedures and requirements
- line managers may feel threatened by the work of the 'staff' specialists
- communication slows down due to the increasingly complex structure.

> Organisation charts can date quickly, and do not show informal communication structures.

The traditional **organisation chart** outlines a formal structure such as shown by line, or line and staff, organisations. It illustrates the degree of **specialisation** in the firm, indicates the layers of **hierarchy**, and defines individual roles. It also provides a summary of a formal structure, which can be used in induction training and which acts as a record of changes and developments.

Matrix organisational structure

Today, many organisations have reduced the number of layers in their hierarchy, restructuring to take the emphasis away from functions and towards operations, projects, or tasks. This matrix structure is associated with firms that have a **task culture**, which is project-oriented and focuses on achieving given tasks or jobs.

> These firms are often working in fast-changing markets, selling products or services with relatively short life-cycles (e.g. telecommunications).

The matrix structure combines the use of line departments with **project** (task) **teams** which have been drawn from the various line functions according to task requirements. These may be temporary in nature, or they may have a permanent brief to follow. Although some team members may face a clash of loyalties, there are a number of advantages of the matrix approach:

- team membership, and the authority to carry out projects and tasks, are determined more by individual ability than by formal position and rank
- traditional departmental barriers are broken down
- motivation is increased through varied work (e.g. moving to a new team/task)
- the limitation of only line managers working together is overcome.

> However, overall control becomes more complex, and some team members may face a clash of loyalties between the task and their own department.

> **KEY POINT**
>
> The matrix structure is most effective in firms having wide spans of control and comparatively few hierarchical levels of responsibility.

Progress check

1 Identify two ways in which a company may use an organisation chart.
2 Distinguish between role and task cultures.

2 Role focuses on person's job role; task focuses on firm's projects.
1 To review existing lines of communication; for induction training.

3.2 Features of organisational structure

After studying this section you should be able to:

- explain how these terms relate to organisational structure: delayering, span of control, chain of command
- assess benefits associated with (a) centralisation and (b) decentralisation
- explain the importance to a firm of effective delegation

LEARNING SUMMARY

The five key features

AQA	M2
EDEXCEL	M1
OCR	M2, M3
WJEC	M1, M4
NICCEA	M2

> A major side-effect may be increased pressure and stress on the staff involved.

Delayering

An organisation may seek to reduce the number of layers in its hierarchy, restructuring through delayering, i.e. removing one or more layers of the firm's management hierarchy. Delayering may be implemented to:

- increase spans of control (which become wider as a result of the delayering);
- reduce communication problems (and related costs).

> Following his appointment, Manfred Halper implemented a programme to restructure the Plumbing business for growth. These changes have eliminated an entire layer of management and made the business more market and consumer focused, as well as removing unnecessary costs and duplication.
>
> *Delta plc annual report and accounts 1998 (extract)*

Span of control

This can be defined as the number of subordinates directly under the control of a manager. It is described as **wide** when the manager has many subordinates, and **narrow** when the manager has few subordinates. The width of an individual's span of control is influenced by three principal factors:

> Too narrow a span leads to over-supervision, denying staff the chance to show initiative: too wide a span means lack of control and the chance of costly mistakes.

1 the degree of complexity of the work involved – simple tasks that are easily supervised are associated with wide spans, and more complex or advanced work with narrow spans

2 the level of staff skill and ability – well-trained and able employees can be supervised efficiently in larger groups compared with new or untrained staff

3 the manager's own level of ability and training.

By widening the span of control:

- delegation is encouraged (the manager has less time for each subordinate)
- fewer layers of hierarchy are now required, thereby improving the speed of communication between top and bottom of the hierarchy.

By narrowing the span of control:

- there may be less pressure on employees
- closer management supervision is possible, which may be important in certain industries (e.g. where safety is at a premium).

> **KEY POINT**
>
> A narrow span of control is most suited to straightforward tasks: a wide span, since it reduces supervision, is more associated with delegation.

Chain of command

This establishes how **power** and **control** are passed downwards through an organisation. The chain becomes more complicated as the organisation's size increases: where a sole trader may liaise with all employees, large companies have chains of command that go through a number of layers of authority.

Organisational structures can be analysed into **tall** and **flat** forms. Tall structures indicate long chains of command. As a result:

As a general rule, the taller the structure, the larger the firm.

- high-level decisions can take a long time to reach employees at the bottom of the chain, and to be actioned
- there may be a 'them and us' feeling of remoteness between those at both ends of the chain
- this feeling is reinforced by the formal communication systems and methods associated with tall structures
- spans of control are often narrow
- employees are usually highly task-specialised.

> **KEY POINT**
>
> Flat structures are increasingly popular nowadays and are associated with smaller organisations and shorter chains of command.

Centralisation

When applied to organisational structures, the **degree of centralisation influences the authority to make decisions**. Centralisation allows managers to make and communicate quickly decisions which are consistent across the organisation. However, a highly centralised structure denies those lower down the chain of command the power or the authority to make decisions for themselves. As an illustration, many well-known 'fast food' outlets operating as franchises have little if any scope regarding display, pricing policy and the style or amount of advertising. The benefit is that customers have a virtual guarantee that every McDonald's or Wimpy outlet will be broadly the same. Another typical example of centralised organisations is the 'multiple' retailer, where counter layout, prices, promotions and window displays are determined without the direct involvement of individual store staff.

This term is also used to identify whether an organisation's services, such as reprographics, are organised on a centralised or decentralised basis.

> Marks & Spencer has outgrown the highly centralised structure which drove much of our past expansion and success. While retaining the efficiencies and scale of a large organisation, we are radically restructuring our business to become more responsive to the needs of our customer.
>
> - For the first time our UK Retail business will be managed as a whole, rather than along product lines.
> - We are streamlining central management and giving store and regional managers more control over operating decisions.
> - We are uniting the organisation's extensive knowledge of our customers into a single marketing function.
> - We are establishing clearer lines of accountability, empowering individuals at the point of best expertise and, where possible, measuring staff performance by results.
> - We are pursuing efficiencies by re-examining our buying processes, space requirements, IT and logistics.
>
> *Marks & Spencer plc annual review 1999 (extract)*

Decentralised structures are increasingly popular. They are associated with greater authority at 'unit' (e.g. shop) level and are said to:

- allow a quicker and more effective local response to local needs and conditions
- improve employee motivation through greater involvement in the decision-making process
- lead to more effective **management by objectives** (MBO) through decentralised and personally-devised objectives being set
- lead to better **management by exception** by more accurate budgeting and an improved control system through the use of variances (see page 85).

Delegation

> The key to successful delegation is **mutual trust**.

A manager may delegate – pass down – certain powers to subordinates. The success of delegation is influenced by the responsibility, authority and accountability of those involved with the tasks.

Responsibility

If employees are to carry out tasks delegated to them, they must accept the responsibility for carrying out the tasks, and therefore for any failure. As a result, the responsibilities must be **identified** clearly, **recorded** (e.g. in the job description), and **reasonable** in nature and scope given the subordinate's training, qualifications and experience.

Authority

The employee who will carry out the delegated work must be given the authority to do so. This authority might have to be **communicated** to others, such as another manager who is holding information to which the employee would not normally have access.

Accountability

> A side-benefit of delegation is that it results in the junior employee taking on additional responsibilities, therefore being trained for later advancement.

Delegation correctly given results in the subordinate being accountable to the manager – and, in turn, the manager to the next person up the chain of command – for the success of the work.

An organisation suffers when delegation has been unsuccessful: this normally occurs where the work delegated is unsuitable (e.g. too complex or specialised), the delegator may have difficulty in delegating due to unwillingness to relinquish tasks, or the subordinate may lack adequate training, confidence or motivation.

> **KEY POINT**
>
> Delegation is associated with larger organisations, simply because no one person can effectively control all the functions of such a firm.

Progress check

1 Distinguish between 'span of control' and 'chain of command'.

2 What are the benefits to managers and subordinates from successful delegation?

2 Managers have reduced workload, can focus on key tasks, and make better decisions; subordinates gain more experience, and are more highly motivated.

1 Span of control: number of subordinates under a person's control. Chain of command: the flow of control (down) and information (up and down) through the organisation.

3.3 Communication in the organisation

After studying this section you should be able to:

- *outline the role of business communication*
- *identify key oral and written communication methods used in firms*
- *explain the major barriers to effective communication in organisations*

The role of business communication

AQA	A2
EDEXCEL	M1
OCR	A2
WJEC	A2
NICCEA	A2

Business communication **transmits information** through the hierarchy/chain of command. This transmission takes place via **communication channels**. The formal channels are indicated by the firm's formal structure, shown by the **vertical** chains of command in its organisation chart. **Horizontal** communication channels also exist: for example, communication taking place at team meetings where the team is drawn from a number of departments. A channel may be either 'open' – to all in the firm, e.g. via a noticeboard – or 'closed', where the communication is limited to named individuals or roles.

> Most managers recognise the value of informal channels due to their typically positive effect on employee morale and motivation.

Informal communication channels co-exist with formal ones. They can assume great importance in firms with tall structures, and where the formal channels are not working efficiently.

Managers need to make decisions concerning:

- the nature of the communication – e.g. whether formal or informal
- any special skills required to communicate the information efficiently – e.g. knowledge of how an e-mail system operates
- the methods available – e.g. whether to use oral or written forms.

Oral communication is most valuable for transmitting basic, low-volume information quickly. It has the advantage over written forms of being an immediate two-way process, though given the instantaneous nature of fax and e-mail, this advantage is less important nowadays. It may be informal (e.g. a telephone call) or formal, such as in a business meeting or an interview.

Written communication is widely used where high-volume and/or technical information needs transmitting, and has the major advantage that a written record of the communication is available if required. A manager will typically choose a memorandum as an informal form; popular formal written communication methods include reports, letters and technical manuals.

Joint ventures

The Group operates several businesses as joint ventures with external partners including property joint ventures and Tesco Personal Finance, our financial services joint venture. The total share of profits of our joint ventures was £6m (1998 – loss of £6m).

Tesco Personal Finance has been an important part of our business strategy now for two years and is in good shape. Products launched to date, including savings, loans, visa, insurance and pensions have all been popular and over one million customers now use our financial services.

Extract from Tesco plc annual report, 1999.

Computers form the backbone of most communication systems. Advantages of their use include: improved quality/readability (e.g. laser printers); reduced costs of storing, manipulating and transmitting information; and greater security of stored information.

Barriers to effective communication

AQA	A2
EDEXCEL	M1
OCR	A2
WJEC	A2
NICCEA	A2

The transmitter:

- uses an inappropriate level of language, e.g. jargon or complex technical terms
- selects inaccurate language
- uses poor sentence structure
- omits important information
- makes inappropriate non-verbal signals in supporting the message.

The message:

- is sent using inappropriate methods
- goes through an over-long chain of command
- contains a high level of 'redundancy' (the amount of information being transmitted is far more than required).

The medium:

- is unsuitable for the information being transmitted
- is too slow in getting the message to the recipient for action.

The recipient:

- may choose to ignore the message
- is in an unsuitable physical or emotional state to receive it
- interprets the message incorrectly, e.g. due to personal bias.

Most communication suffers from 'noise', which can be either background noise, or some other distraction such as faulty equipment.

Systems analysis can be used to evaluate the efficiency of the present structure, and systems design undertaken to develop improved procedures and routines for the organisation.

Overcoming the barriers

Managers must seek to overcome these barriers. The quality of staff training in communication procedures and techniques will need reviewing; communication media need evaluating for clarity and suitability; and the complexity of the organisational structure must be studied.

Progress check

1 Give two examples of (a) formal, and (b) informal, communication.

2 Why does the growth in a firm's size often cause communications to deteriorate?

2 Larger size extends the channels of communication and chain networks: there are more layers of hierarchy through which the message must pass.

1 Formal: oral presentation to a group of managers; minutes of a meeting. Informal: talk about work at lunch break; informal Quality Circle meeting.

3.4 Size and growth

After studying this section you should be able to:

- state and evaluate the main ways of measuring a firm's size
- explain the difference between internal and external growth
- assess the merits of horizontal, vertical and lateral forms of integration
- explain why firms divest or demerge

Measuring size

AQA	M2
EDEXCEL	M1
OCR	M1
WJEC	M1
NICCEA	M3

The size of an organisation can be measured using different indicators. Some are more suitable than others, depending on the nature of the organisation.

Turnover

The level of annual sales is the most widely used indicator of a firm's size: it indicates ability to obtain finance and to benefit from economies of scale. Limitations of using turnover as the measure of size include:

- turnover often varies greatly from year to year
- since profit margins vary between industries, firms having similar turnover figures may have quite different profits
- turnover is not necessarily an indicator of market share or market value.

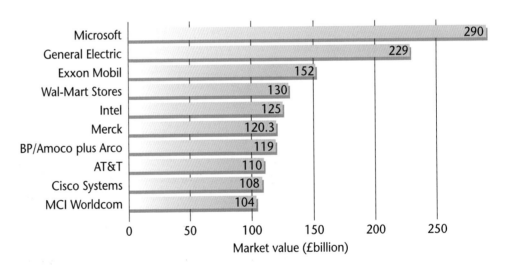

Figure 3.2 *The world's largest companies by market value (£billion), 1999*

Capital employed

Capital employed shows net investment and is compared with profit to assess profitability. It can be a difficult figure to measure: firms in the same industry may use different bases for valuing assets, which affects capital employed figures and leads to inaccurate comparisons.

Profits

A firm's profit figure – such as profit before tax – may be used to indicate its size. One drawback of using this measure is that different firms in the same industry will operate on different profit margins.

Employees

This is often a straightforward indicator to use, but firms in different industries will have differing capital/labour ratios: for example, a service sector firm is normally much more labour-intensive than one in the manufacturing sector.

> Firms in the same industry should be compared using the same indicator of size.
>
> **KEY POINT**

Profits before tax	Turnover		Capital employed	Employees
£ million	£ million		£ million	
(1) Delta 40.3	(1) Glynwed 1,015	**MANUFACTURERS** Delta Glynwed	(1) Glynwed 334.5	(1) Delta 15,383
(2) Glynwed 36.4	(2) Delta 663		(2) Delta 315.3	(2) Glynwed 11,624
(1) Tesco 842	(1) Tesco 17,158	**RETAILERS** Tesco Sainsbury's	(1) Sainsbury 4,663	(1) Sainsbury 177,906
(2) Sainsbury 832	(2) Sainsbury 15,196		(2) Tesco 4,377	(2) Tesco 172,712

Figure 3.3 *Comparisons of size*
Source: annual accounts of Glynwed plc and Delta plc (1998), and J Sainsbury plc and Tesco plc (1999)

Methods of growth

AQA — M2
EDEXCEL — M2
OCR — M2
WJEC — M5
NICCEA — M3

Size (number of employees)	Number of Businesses	Employment (000s)	Turnover (£millions)	Business (%)	Employment (%)	Turnover (%)
None	2,339,645	2,749	88,634	64.0	12.7	4.6
1–4	922,585	2,356	214,258	25.2	10.9	11.1
5–9	204,290	1,483	123,017	5.6	6.9	6.4
10–19	111,800	1,568	154,360	3.1	7.3	8.0
20–49	48,300	1,496	152,716	1.3	6.9	7.9
50–99	14,945	1,043	110,925	0.4	4.8	5.8
100–199	8,145	1,127	116,995	0.2	5.2	6.1
200–249	1,520	338	37,781	–	1.6	2.0
250–499	3,215	1,123	154,639	0.1	5.2	8.0
500+	3,445	8,311	773,663	0.1	38.5	40.1
All	3,657,885	21,595	1,926,987	100.0	100.0	100.0
All with employee(s)	1,318,240	18,846	1,838,353	36.0	87.3	95.4

Figure 3.4 *SME statistics. Number of businesses, employment and turnover by size of enterprise, start 1998*
Source: DTI, 1999

Most firms try to grow in size for specific reasons. Larger size brings with it:

- improved survival prospects through larger market share, diversification into different markets, and greater finance;
- economies of scale (see page 56);
- an increased feeling of status and power.

Internal growth

Also known as organic growth, this occurs when a firm expands, using its own resources by:

> retaining its profits
>
> ↓
>
> preserving its liquid assets
>
> ↓
>
> using them to invest in additional fixed assets
>
> ↓
>
> improving its productive capacity
>
> ↓
>
> increasing its market share and growth

Integration

> A **takeover** occurs when one firm obtains a controlling interest in another: it does not normally involve agreement between the firms.
>
> A **merger** takes place when two (or more) companies agree to combine their assets: the companies are completely reorganised as a result of the merger.

External growth, or integration, occurs when one firm takes over or merges with another. In the UK economy, takeovers and mergers are a popular way for firms to increase in size very quickly.

Horizontal integration occurs when firms making similar products or providing similar services join together. The car industry provides many recent examples: General Motors acquired Isuzu; Ford acquired Mazda; Volkswagen acquired Skoda; Toyota acquired Daihatsu.

	FORD	VOLVO		BP	AMOCO
Founded	1903	1927	Founded	1901	1889
Founded by	Henry Ford	Assar Gabrielson Gustaf Larson	Employees	56,000	43,000
			Petrol stations	17,900	9,300
Turnover	£72.7bn (1998)	£7.6bn (1997)	Annual revenues	£44.4bn	£22.5bn
Company value	£44bn	£7.3bn	Barrels of oil pumped per day	3.3 million	1.2 million
Employees	364,000	28,000	Market worth	£46.3 bn	£24.1 bn

Figure 3.5 *The Ford/Volvo and BP/Amoco links.*   *Source: annual reports, 1999*

Because horizontal integration involves firms in the same industry at the same stage of production, the results should be larger-scale production and economies of scale. The new company will have a greater market dominance since it now has the previous market share of the former companies: in saturated markets this could be the only way to increase substantially market share.

Companies in the same industry may decide to establish links rather than join formally. Such joint ventures:

- avoid the expense and permanent commitment of a formal merger
- help to reduce competition
- improve competitiveness through sharing resources and expertise.

Vertical integration occurs when two firms in the same industry but at different stages of production amalgamate. Vertical forwards integration is when a firm amalgamates with one of its outlets, for example when an oil company acquires a chain of petrol stations. Vertical backwards integration is when a firm moves back down the production chain and obtains one of its suppliers (e.g. a food processing firm taking over an agricultural producer).

Motives for vertical integration include:

- **protection** – by the firm controlling its outlets or suppliers
- **control** – the firm now has closer control over quality, delivery and levels of supply, as well as greater control of its market
- **profits** – the profits of the previous supplier/outlet now belong to the firm, allowing greater flexibility on pricing and profit margins.

Lateral integration

Also known as **conglomerate** or **diversified** integration, this occurs when firms in different industries and markets amalgamate. There may be some link between the firms' products, or the conglomerate may own quite different companies.

> An example is British American Tobacco, diversifying to counter the contracting UK market for smokers' products.

The main advantage of lateral integration is **diversification**, i.e. not over-relying on a single product or market. Risk is spread over different products and markets: failure in one area should not lead to collapse. Also, companies that were in a saturated market are no longer limited by that market.

Arguments against integration

- **Reduced competitiveness** – the growth resulting from integration may cause diseconomies of scale (see page 57).
- **Asset stripping** – a predator company acquires another firm because it believes the market value of the firm's assets is greater than the firm's stock market valuation: the predator then closes the bought firm to sell off the assets.
- **Over-borrowing** – increased financial costs (e.g. interest payments on loans taken out to finance the acquisition) may affect the company's profitability.

Deintegration

> Reasons for demerging include a failure to achieve expected economies of scale, and the need to cut costs (e.g. in times of economic turndown).

A company might reduce the scope of its activities. The main reason is financial: raising finance through selling a subsidiary, or cutting costs through the drive for efficiency. Deintegration occurs through **divestment** – selling a subsidiary that no longer fits into the company's long-term strategy – or **demerger**, where an existing company is split into two or more new groups/divisions.

> The resources to accomplish this transformation have been generated through selling our long-established metals business ... Divestments have provided resources for subsequent acquisitions ... after the sale of its metals distribution business in May, the Group was able to acquire the leading German pipe systems company ... We then reverted to divestment ... and we shall now return to the acquisition process.
>
> *Glynwed plc annual report and accounts, 1998 (extract)*

Progress check

1 Name **four** methods of measuring the size of a firm.
2 What is the difference between horizontal and vertical integration?

2 Horizontal: between firms in the same market and at the same stage of production. Vertical: between firms in the same market but at different stages of production.

1 Turnover; profits; capital employed; number of employees.

3.5 Economies of scale

After studying this section you should be able to:

- *appreciate how scale affects a firm's costs*
- *describe the different types of internal and external economies of scale*
- *explain why managers must be aware of diseconomies of scale*

LEARNING SUMMARY

Internal economies of scale

AQA	M2
EDEXCEL	M2
OCR	M2
WJEC	M5
NICCEA	M3

These are created when a firm's **unit cost of production falls as output and its scale of operation increases**. The increased volume of production does not normally increase fixed costs (see page 92): these costs are spread over a larger output, and as a result the average cost per unit falls.

Economies of increased dimensions

These arise from an increase in size: for example, supertankers can carry many times the cargo volume compared to traditional tankers, more than offsetting their increased running costs.

Financial economies

Larger firms are assumed to be more stable financially, and therefore find it easier to obtain loan capital. They can negotiate lower interest rates on these loans. Larger companies (PLCs) also have more, often less expensive, sources of finance available.

> The principle of **division of labour** leads to a greater efficiency in specialist areas.

Managerial economies

Growth in the firm's size leads to employment of specialist managers, bringing greater levels of expertise to the firm.

Marketing economies

Larger firms can buy the services of specialist marketing companies such as advertising agencies. A wider range of promotion is possible, with the extra cost being spread over more sales, reducing the unit cost of promotion.

Purchasing economies

Larger firms can take advantage of bulk-buying discounts, thereby reducing unit material costs. They can also negotiate more favourable credit terms with suppliers.

Risk-bearing economies

Firms grow larger through increasing their product range. This diversification spreads risk over more products and markets.

Technical economies

A larger firm can afford research and development costs, which may lead to improved products or savings from technological breakthroughs. The use of efficient, sophisticated technological equipment can often only be met by the larger organisations.

> These economies are measurable financially: they can normally be quantified.

KEY POINT

External economies of scale

For example, Japanese language courses are offered in Telford, which is the West Midlands home for many Japanese multinationals.

These arise from a growth in the size of the **industry**, and all firms in the industry benefit from these economies. External economies have often been found where the industry is/was concentrated in a particular area.

Support

Local firms provide specialist services, such as car component manufacturers in the Midlands supplying the local car industry.

Training

Firms also benefit from an area's good reputation, e.g. 'Sheffield steel'.

Employees improve skills via local training providers supplying industry-specific courses. This skilled pool of labour is available to all firms in the area.

Information

Examples include making china in the Potteries, shipbuilding in the north-east, and financial services in London.

Local trade associations and chambers of commerce develop and provide specialist information.

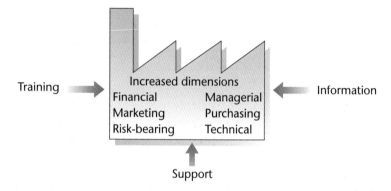

Figure 3.6 *Internal and external economies of scale*

Diseconomies of scale

AQA	M2
EDEXCEL	M2
OCR	M2
WJEC	M5
NICCEA	M3

Communication may also become distorted, leading to a further increase in inefficiency.

There are practical limits to the growth that can take place. Beyond a certain point, an organisation finds that its **unit costs increase**: it starts to suffer from diseconomies of scale. These diseconomies arise for a number of reasons. The larger the firm, the more levels of hierarchy there tend to be for communication to flow through, leading to greater bureaucracy. This results in:

- worker dissatisfaction and poor labour relations, which in turn cause low morale, higher absenteeism, or actions such as overtime bans
- the chain of command lengthening, with decisions becoming slower to implement, which
  - reduces efficiency and therefore raises costs
  - means the firm is slower to react to changing (e.g. market) conditions.

> These diseconomies are not as quantitative as economies of scale, being more qualitative in nature.
>
> **KEY POINT**

Progress check

1 What is the difference between internal and external economies of scale?

2 Why must managers be aware of diseconomies of scale?

2 Unit costs and inefficiency increase, making the firm less competitive.

1 Internal: based within the firm. External: available to all firms in the area.

Sample questions and model answers

1

Since large size brings so many benefits to a firm, explain how small firms continue to survive. [6]

The examiner will expect you to show your knowledge of the particular nature of small firms.

There are two main reasons why small firms continue to survive.

First, the firm may supply a local or limited market. It may provide a personal service, such as hairdressing or plumbing, provide convenience (such as the local 'corner shop'), or it may operate in a small segment of the market, such as domestic building extensions and improvements. It can compete successfully because the demand for its product or service is likely to be limited, for example where it is in a specialist or luxury market.

Second, the policy of the owner(s) may be to stay small. This may be due to reasons such as a lack of ambition, the desire to remain in charge, or the wish to avoid what is seen as unnecessary risk. The owner(s) may be attracted by the nature of entrepreneurship: in such cases, the level of profits is not as important as it may be to a larger firm having external demands (e.g. shareholder expectations) to meet.

It can be useful to provide a summary showing your knowledge of the overall situation.

Small firms have a number of typical strengths which help them to survive. They are quicker to respond to market forces; communication between all levels tends to be efficient, and labour relations are often very good.

2

How might economies of scale be useful to a vehicle manufacturer? [6]

You can start with an overall definition, to show your basic understanding of the term.

'Economies of scale' refers to the unit cost savings that are made as firms grow in size. Although total costs will increase, these are proportionately lower than the increase in output, because fixed costs do not automatically increase as output increases. Economies of scale may be internal to the firm, e.g. bulk-buying discounts which lower the price of materials, or external (e.g. improved provision of local training).

Remember the examiners now expect you to apply your general knowledge of economies of scale to the given situation.

An example of an internal economy of scale from which a vehicle manufacturer might benefit is the purchasing economy mentioned above. Other likely economies are financial (lower interest rates on loans for new machinery), marketing (spreading the cost of advertising over higher output can make TV advertising of the vehicles cost-effective), managerial (specialists in vehicle research, development, manufacture and sale can be employed), and technical (shopfloor employees can use specially developed machinery and equipment making production more efficient).

Practice examination question

Fizzy Drinks plc produces a range of six soft drinks at five different plants throughout the UK. Two of the products are well-established; the other four have been introduced within the last four years. Two of these new products have produced disappointing results. The Marketing Manager has complained to the Managing Director that the Operations Manager, one of whose departments is Research and Development, has not responded to a series of memos outlining consumer dissatisfaction with these products. The Operations Manager has responded that his department is fully stretched trying to co-ordinate production on five different sites.

The board of directors has commissioned a firm of management consultants to advise them on the possible restructuring of the organisation of the company. The preliminary report of the management consultants stated that the span of control seems too narrow.

Here is the current organisational chart of Fizzy Drinks plc.

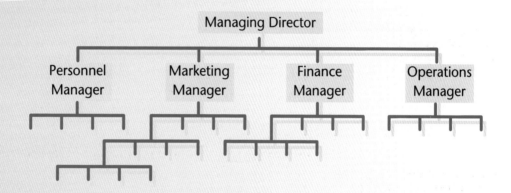

(a) Analyse the problems, resulting from a narrow span of control, which could be created for large-scale manufacturing firms like Fizzy Drinks. [8]

(b) State possible reasons why there is conflict between the Marketing and Operations Manager and evaluate possible solutions for this problem. [10]

(c) Discuss alternative structures which a firm producing a range of soft drinks on several sites might introduce and recommend what you consider to be the most appropriate structure. [8]

Edexcel Specimen Unit 1 Q3

Chapter 4

External influences

The following topics are covered in this chapter:

- *Macro-economic issues*
- *Government support*
- *Legal regulation*
- *Other influences*

4.1 Macro-economic issues

After studying this section you should be able to:

- *explain how the business cycle affects firms in different ways*
- *identify how interest and exchange rates affect business operations*
- *analyse the effect of inflation on business*
- *comment on the different types of unemployment*

LEARNING SUMMARY

The business cycle

AQA	M3
EDEXCEL	M1
OCR	M1
WJEC	M1
NICCEA	M1

Figure 4.1 shows how this cycle operates.

Stage	Firms
Recession: contracting output; gloomy outlook	experience falling demand and so cut prices and dismiss staff; losses are made; investment falls; some go out of business.
Recovery: the economy starts expanding; rising, but limited, expectations	experience increase in demand; review their employment and investment positions but still lack confidence.
Boom: rapid growth in output; high confidence but fear of inflation	invest and take on staff; may find skill shortages; increase prices and profit margins; utilise spare capacity.
Downturn (recession): growth slows again	experience falling demand and profits; start reducing output and investment.

Figure 4.1 *Stages in the business cycle*

Effect on firms

> A benefit of surviving through a recession is that the firm has been forced to examine and overcome some of the weakness in its product range, expertise, organisation, etc.

In the cycle, personal consumption normally fluctuates less than business investment. This affects firms in different ways when a recession or **slump** – a time of falling real incomes – occurs:

- a firm producing **capital equipment** (machinery, etc.) will be badly affected by the reduced investment undertaken by other firms
- firms making and selling **consumer durables** will also be badly hit, since consumers normally postpone replacing these items until an economic upturn occurs and they are more confident about employment and income

> Firms that have **diversified** are in a stronger position to survive recessions.

- firms making and selling **basic necessities** will experience less of a fall in demand – it may increase, as consumers switch expenditure away from luxuries onto these items.

Interest rates

AQA	M3
EDEXCEL	M1
OCR	M1
WJEC	M1
NICCEA	M1

> The theory is that more growth means more inflation, and more inflation means higher interest rates.

An interest rate indicates the cost of borrowing money: from the lender's viewpoint it is the cost of not having the money available, or 'lost liquidity'. Interest rates and borrowing decisions are influenced by **opportunity cost**: for the borrower this is the cost of not taking out the loan (i.e. going without the item bought by the loan), and for the lender it is not having the cash to spend.

The level of interest rates is therefore important for firms and individuals, which is why governments regard manipulating interest rates as a key tool of economic policy.

> If interest rates are increased, borrowing – and so spending – will fall, taking demand-led pressure out of the economy and reducing inflation. Firms face not only the direct cost of increased interest payments, but also a falling demand for their goods and services.

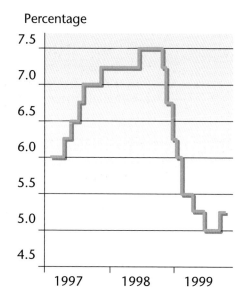

Figure 4.2 *UK interest rates, 1997–1999*

Exchange rates

AQA	M3
EDEXCEL	M1
OCR	M1
WJEC	M1
NICCEA	M1

Chapter 1 explained the nature of exchange rates. Fluctuating exchange rates cause importers and exporters concern, and may even discourage an entrepreneur from establishing an overseas market for the firm's products.

A rising exchange rate means:

- for an **importer**, lower costs for imported items
- for an **exporter**, reduced price-competitiveness and profit margins.

Falling exchange rates similarly benefit exporters but disadvantage importers.

Exchange rates therefore affect business decision-making. Entrepreneurs seek to increase profit margins, by increasing sales/selling prices and/or cutting costs. The choice of where to sell and where to buy from is influenced by exchange rate fluctuations. **Multinationals** are in a stronger position to cope with these fluctuations, compared with firms based only in a single country, because they can move resources and accounting procedures from country to country in order to take advantage of these fluctuations.

> **KEY POINT**
>
> Firms find it difficult to remain competitive with exchange rates altering. Exporters must consider whether to change price or accept different profit margins, and importers whether to maintain overseas or home sources of supply, depending on how the rate has changed.

Inflation

AQA	M3
EDEXCEL	M1
OCR	M1
WJEC	M1
NICCEA	M1

Inflation is defined as a persistent tendency for prices to rise over time. Because of the effect of inflation on firms and people, its control becomes a high priority for any government. Most western governments (including the UK) believe that economies have 'speed limits': output cannot grow at full speed without causing price rises.

Causes of inflation

Cost-push inflation occurs when production costs increase, perhaps due to pay rises not being supported by productivity increases, or through costs of imported items rising due to the pound falling on the foreign exchange market.

Demand-pull inflation occurs when aggregate (total) demand in the economy exceeds aggregate supply. Governments attempt to control this inflation through **monetary policy** – controlling credit by reducing its availability or increasing its cost – and by **fiscal policy**, increasing taxation to reduce spending power or cutting government spending to reduce demand.

The fall in high-street prices in the late 1990s – in 1999 the price of consumer durables fell by up to 3.5% year on year – is an example of **'entrenched deflation'**.

Deflation occurs when this downward pressure on economic activity produces falling demand and prices: the danger is that, as a result, firms reduce output and employment. Deflation can also cause problems for the government. For example, state pensions have been linked to the RPI (see below). In times of falling prices it would be politically impossible to reduce pensions: maintaining the level of pensions would put the government's finances under pressure.

> **Inflation targeting** is carried out by the UK government: a target inflation level is set, and the Bank of England helps manipulate interest rates to meet this target. Through the 1990s the target rate was 2.5%.
>
> **KEY POINT**

Measuring inflation

In the 1990s the UK's inflation fell steeply from the 1991 figure of over 5% to a 36-year low of 1.1% by late 1999.

A popular measure of inflation is the **retail prices index** (RPI). The prices of a representative sample of purchases made by households – the average 'shopping basket' – are weighted in importance and recorded. The index is calculated against a base year. Other measures of inflation include the 'factory gate' indicator of the price of firms' inputs.

These indicators have their limitations. For example, the RPI is based on the average shopping basket: but many people who rely on RPI figures for increases in their income may have quite different spending patterns, with their increased costs not reflecting those shown by RPI calculations.

The importance of inflation

Entrepreneurs have **inflationary expectations**, their business plans being influenced by what they expect to happen to inflation in the future. The actions they take as a result may help fulfil these expectations: for example, if the rate of inflation is expected to increase, entrepreneurs may buy goods now, increasing present demand levels and reinforcing any demand-pull inflation. Their employees may seek higher wage increases on the basis of the expected rise in inflation, increasing costs and adding to any cost-push inflation in the economy.

Inflation affects firms' **behaviour** and chances of **survival**. Long-term planning becomes more difficult; profit margins may be squeezed, since firms cannot always pass prices on (if they do, their selling prices become uncompetitive); the increase in interest rates during inflationary periods hits firms with high debt borrowing and may encourage them to pay higher dividends (which reduces their cash levels); and UK exporters may find the increase in their prices due to inflation makes them uncompetitive overseas.

Inflation also hits those on a fixed income such as pensioners – though indexing of pensions may counter this – and will therefore affect the demand level for firms supplying these consumers. It may also distort general economic behaviour (high inflation often encourages saving and reduces spending, leading to an economic downturn – low inflation tends to encourage spending and fuels output and recovery).

Firms may **benefit** from inflation: for example, those with high borrowing find that the sum owed is falling in real terms, making it easier to repay the loan at the end of its life.

> There is evidence that the UK's recent low inflation rate is kept low partly by increased **globalisation**, which has led to increased competition.

> The action of firms can also counter inflation: an example is where cut-throat competition occurs, such as the 'price war' amongst supermarkets in 1999, triggered by Wal-Mart's takeover of Asda.

Unemployment

AQA	M3
EDEXCEL	M1
OCR	M1
WJEC	M1
NICCEA	M1

Full employment is another typical key government objective (although there are various ways of interpreting what is meant by 'full'). Unemployment can be:

- **structural** – where industries face structural decline through lack of competitiveness: for example, the old 'staple' industries such as shipbuilding and mining (see below). This has badly affected these areas, and continues with the trend towards **de-industrialisation**

- **frictional** – caused by the time lag between moving from one job to another. It is linked to labour's **geographical immobility** where a person will not move to another area (e.g. the high cost of housing in south-east England), and its **occupational immobility** (e.g. lack of skill to do the jobs available)

- **casual** or **seasonal** – found in sectors such as agriculture and tourism

- **cyclical** – due to downturn in the business cycle.

Structural changes in particular in the economy lead to expansion of some sectors and/or areas at the expense of others, and these changes influence employment patterns. Unemployment rates vary considerably across the UK. Areas that used to rely on heavy industries and which have since declined often have some of the highest rates of unemployment. For example, Cleveland and Merseyside were traditionally strong shipbuilding areas before this industry experienced a decline, and South Yorkshire was a prosperous coal-mining region. By spring 1998 these areas had unemployment rates well above the UK average, at 7.3, 10.9 and 9.6 per cent, respectively (*source: ONS, 1999*).

Progress check

1 Distinguish between interest and exchange rates.
2 What is the difference between cost-push and demand-pull inflation?

1 Interest rates determine the cost of borrowing money. Exchange rates involve the relative cost of currency.
2 Cost-push: based on higher input (production) costs being translated into higher prices. Demand-pull: occurs when the demand for goods exceeds their supply.

4.2 Government support

After studying this section you should be able to:

- *summarise how government influences a firm's decisions*
- *explain the reasons for government support for industry*
- *outline how the DTI and other agencies support industry*

Areas of influence

AQA	M3
EDEXCEL	M1
OCR	M1
WJEC	M1
NICCEA	M1

Local and central government, together with the European Union, influence a firm's decisions regarding its:

- **location**: e.g. granting planning permission, creating the Single Market
- **workforce**: e.g. passing employee protection and health and safety legislation, allowing free movement of labour in the EU
- **trade links**: e.g. removing tariff barriers, giving help to exporters
- **expansion**: e.g. passing legislation controlling monopolies and mergers
- **income**: e.g. altering tax rates
- **finance**: e.g. influencing the level of interest rates.

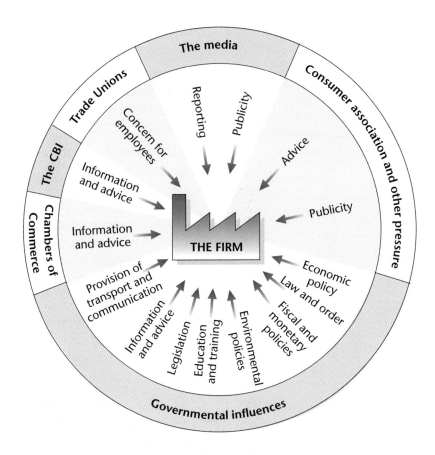

Figure 4.3 *External influences on a firm*

Governments seek both to control and to help the various sections of the economy. The UK government, in order to meet its key economic and social objectives, works with the EU to support economic development.

UK government support

AQA	M3
EDEXCEL	M1
OCR	M1
WJEC	M1
NICCEA	M1

The UK government, together with the EU, has a number of key economic objectives. These are normally based on controlling **inflation** (page 62), having a stable **balance of payments**, and fighting **unemployment**: government policies are designed to achieve set objectives in these areas. The government also tries to make its economy compete successfully with other competitor economies in the global marketplace (see Figure 8.1, page 121).

The Department of Trade and Industry (DTI)

The DTI supports UK industry in many ways. An example of how it does this is the **Business Link** support network, operated by the DTI in partnership with chambers of commerce, local authorities and Learning and Skills Councils.

Why?

Business Links help businesses compete, develop and grow in an increasingly competitive world marketplace.

How?

By bringing together all the support services available to businesses, Business Links provide the kind of quality help that really counts; how to raise money for growth; how to get into export markets; how to source the most suitable training packages; and how to manage change and help with the full range of issues affecting business.

The Business Link network. Source: Business Link, 1999

The DTI provides other assistance for business:

Specific help for small and new businesses

It operates a Small Business Service; the Small Firms Loan Guarantee Scheme guarantees loans for small businesses that have failed to obtain a loan due to a lack of security.

Improving performance

The DTI also helps with **environmental** matters and **regulations**, and supports **trade associations**.

It provides free booklets and 'best practice' guides; the National Business Improvement Services allow firms to compare their business performance against others.

Expansion

It liaises with over 100 UK export clubs; the Regional Selective Assistance scheme aims to attract investment and create/safeguard jobs in Assisted Areas (see page 66); the Enterprise Fund provides financial support; the DTI supports the National Business Angels Network that brings together companies and potential investors.

Innovation and technology

The Information Society Initiative helps firms take advantage of new computer and communications technologies; the SMART scheme provides grants to develop technologies; the International Technology Service keeps firms aware of developments.

European matters

The DTI's Spearhead database contains data on the Single Market; it provides a series of Product Standards booklets.

Other government support and advice

ONS publications include **Regional Trends, Social Trends** and **Economic Trends.**

- **The Office for National Statistics (ONS)** – this is the government agency responsible for compiling many of the UK's economic and social statistics: firms use this information to analyse market and other trends.
- **British Trade International (BTI)** – this operation provides support information, advice and assistance.
- **The Export Credit Guarantee Department** – the ECGD supports exports by providing guarantees and insurance against loss.

The ECGD covers around £3 billion of UK exports each year.

Providing training and employment schemes

The UK government has developed a range of financial incentives to encourage people to improve their skills. For example, the Department for Education and Employment operates the New Deal training initiative, which provides financial support for salary and training costs.

Implementing a regional policy

The UK government and the EU seek to correct economic imbalances between areas by stimulating the economy in the less well-off areas. This reduces inequality of income and employment, helping firms in these areas compete more effectively, and countering problems of unemployment due to factors such as structural decline (see page 63) and geographical immobility of labour.

In 1999, gross domestic product per head in Wales was only 82% of the UK average.

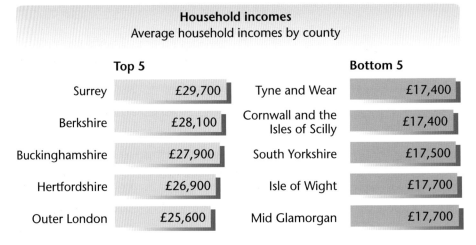

Household incomes
Average household incomes by county

Top 5		Bottom 5	
Surrey	£29,700	Tyne and Wear	£17,400
Berkshire	£28,100	Cornwall and the Isles of Scilly	£17,400
Buckinghamshire	£27,900	South Yorkshire	£17,500
Hertfordshire	£26,900	Isle of Wight	£17,700
Outer London	£25,600	Mid Glamorgan	£17,700

Figure 4.4 UK average household incomes, 1999   _Source: CACI, 1999_

- The Department for Education and Employment helps implement the government's Employment Zones.
- The UK government has offered selective regional financial assistance, e.g. through encouraging firms to settle in development areas (an approach reinforced by the EU's Regional Policy).
- Enterprise zones were set up in areas hit by severe unemployment, and received government grants.
- Assisted areas have been established, with the government offering grants to encourage firms to settle there.

> Government support for (and control of) business undergoes regular change, as governments themselves have to respond to change.

KEY POINT

The European Union

The EU's employment policy is based on employability, entrepreneurship, adaptability and equality of opportunity.

The EU supports national and local government initiatives. Regional financial support is given through the **European Regional Development Fund**, and financial support for training initiatives through the **European Social Fund**, which spent over Ecu 5.6 billion in 1995 in helping people back into work. The EU is committed to internal mobility of labour: for example, barriers to mobility for regulated professions have been removed.

An example of EU support is a financial assistance scheme (the 1998–2000 budget was Ecu 420 million) for small and medium enterprises (SMEs) creating employment.

> Objective: to unlock the job-creating potential of high-growth small businesses, particularly in the field of innovative technology, through increased availability of finance ...
>
> The programme of financial assistance ... consists of three complementary facilities:
>
> - a risk capital scheme ... focused on specific sectors such as information and communication technologies, health care and biotechnology.
>
> - a system of financial contributions for the creation of transnational joint ventures between SMEs within the European Union ... the maximum contribution will be Ecu 100,000 per project.
>
> - a SME guarantee facility ... to increase the availability of loans to small or newly established businesses.
>
> *Source: EU Commission, 1999*

The launch of the Single Market programme in 1985 led to the creation of the **Social Charter**, signed by 11 governments (excluding the UK at the time) in 1989. Since this time:

- a charter of fundamental social rights of workers has been adopted, covering aspects such as health and safety at work, protection of the right to join or not to join a trade union, and setting a maximum for working hours
- a further action programme (1995) covering employment and equality of opportunity for women has been followed
- a 'social chapter' incorporating these principles was agreed at Maastricht.

The **European Works Council Directive**, adopted in 1994, was the first Directive to pass into law under the new procedures.

The **Single Market** remains the greatest assistance provided to competitive firms by the European Union. The objective – to remove trade barriers and allow free access to markets – means that companies have access to a market with a spending power even larger than that of North America.

Progress check

1 Why do governments try to support industry?

2 In what ways can a firm benefit from government assistance?

1 To meet objectives, e.g. full employment; to stay competitive internationally.
2 Financial, e.g. through grants; supply of information, e.g. on technological developments.

4.3 Legal regulation

LEARNING SUMMARY

After studying this section you should be able to:

- outline the main features of consumer and anti-competition law
- explain the effect of consumer legislation on firms
- describe why anti-competitive practices are controlled in the UK and EU

General principles

AQA	M3
EDEXCEL	M1
OCR	M1
WJEC	M1
NICCEA	M1

The UK parliament passes 'home' legislation. In the EU, **Regulations** apply directly in all member states and do not have to be confirmed by national parliaments to be legally binding: if there is conflict between a Regulation and existing national law, the Regulation prevails. **Directives** bind member states, but leave the method of implementation up to national governments.

The main areas of legal regulation affecting firms are in the areas of employee protection (see page 98), employment protection (see page 99), consumer protection, and competition policy.

> **KEY POINT**
>
> Legislation has a two-fold effect on business: it acts as a constraint on firms, and as a framework within which firms operate.

Consumer protection

AQA	M3
EDEXCEL	M1
OCR	M1
WJEC	M1
NICCEA	M1

Consumers enter **contracts** when buying goods or services. To support contract law, UK governments and the EU have a range of consumer protection laws.

UK legislation

- The **Sale and Supply of Goods Act** 1994 consolidated other Acts relating to selling goods. Under this Act, goods must be of satisfactory quality, i.e. fit to be sold. They must also be fit for their intended purpose and – if sold by description – they must match their description. (The 1982 Supply of Goods and Services Act extended the sale of goods legislation to services.)
- The **Trade Descriptions Acts** 1968 and 1972 makes it illegal to give a false oral or written description of a good or service.
- The **Consumer Credit Act** (1974) protects consumers against signing unfair contracts, and requires firms to communicate the rate of interest charged.
- The **Financial Services Act** (1986) ensures that firms lending money or offering financial services are controlled.
- The **Food Safety Act** (1990) consolidates earlier law relating to the supply of food products, and protects consumers against the sale of unfit food.

Certain goods, e.g. milk, must be sold in fixed weight/volume so that prices can be compared.

- The **Weights and Measures Acts** (to 1985) protect consumers by making it an offence to sell goods underweight or short in quantity.

The Office of Fair Trading (OFT)

Established in 1973, the OFT plays a key role in protecting the economic welfare of consumers, and in enforcing UK competition policy. Its main roles are to:

- identify and put right trading practices which are against consumer interests
- regulate the provision of consumer credit
- investigate anti-competitive practices and abuses of market power
- help establish market structures encouraging competitive behaviour.

EU influences

EU Directives in this area seek to establish **common levels of consumer protection** throughout the Union. Some Directives have removed trade barriers, others concentrate on transport arrangements to ensure free movement of goods, while the 'New Approach Directives' control product design and give a 'level playing field' for product safety requirements across the EU.

Education and consumer information	Consumer requirements	Protection of consumers' interests
Product packaging: e.g. – pre-packaged products – quick-frozen foods	**Product safety:** e.g. – general product safety [3] – toy safety [4] – dangerous imitations	**Electronic commerce:** e.g. – legal aspects
Product labelling: e.g. – household appliances – beverages – footwear – tobacco	**Consumer health:** e.g. – food safety – veterinary inspections – genetic modification	**Contracts:** e.g. – contracts away from business premises – unfair contract terms [5] – guarantees
Special indications: e.g. – designation of origin	**Quality of goods and services:** e.g. – cosmetic products – foodstuff quality – quality of the environment	**Transport:** e.g. – package travel [6] – air transport
Price indications: e.g. – foodstuffs [1] – gas and electricity		**Financial and insurance services:** e.g. – electronic payments – consumer credit
Advertising: e.g. – misleading adverts [2] – advertising medicines		**Legal redress:** e.g. – access to justice

Figure 4.5 *The general framework for EU activities in favour of the consumer (* indicates specific numbered example, below)*

1 The **Foodstuff Prices** Directive protects and informs consumers by indicating the retail price and the unit price on foodstuffs sold in bulk or pre-packaged. Producers must indicate the selling price and unit price of foodstuffs.

2 The **Misleading Advertising** Directive protects consumers and competitor firms from the consequences of misleading advertising. This Directive also covers **comparative advertising** (which identifies a competitor or the products of a competitor), and protects firms from being unfairly discredited.

3 The **General Product Safety** Directive requires producers to place only safe products on the market. Producers must also provide consumers with the relevant information to enable them to assess the risks inherent in a product through normal use, where these risks are not immediately obvious.

4 The **Toy Safety** Directive ensures that every toy sold in the EU carries a CE mark: by using this symbol, a manufacturer/importer makes a declaration that a product complies with this Directive.

5 Directive 93/13 covers **unfair contract terms**: for example, Article 5 requires all contracts to be drafted in plain, intelligible language. If there is doubt about a term's meaning, the interpretation most favourable to the consumer prevails.

6 The **Package Travel** Directive sets minimum standards of protection for consumers taking package holidays.

Relevance to business

The effects of consumer legislation on firms are:

- **Protection** – e.g. against comparative advertising which could exploit a trade name or which presents a firm's goods as replicas of goods protected by a trade name.
- **Meeting costs** – e.g. food safety laws requiring hygiene-related costs to be met.
- **Customer satisfaction** – through meeting customer expectations, as well as legal requirements, the firm's products are more saleable.
- **Internal systems** – e.g. firms seek to improve Quality Control, and continue developing a 'quality culture'.

> **KEY POINT**
>
> Firms have become increasingly customer-oriented, using market research and public relations as key departments for providing feedback.

Competition policy

AQA	M3
EDEXCEL	M1
OCR	M1
WJEC	M1
NICCEA	M1

This Article applies where there would be an appreciable effect on EU competition.

In the UK and the EU, monopolies and anti-competitive practices are deemed to be **against the public interest**: prices tend to be higher than in a competitive market, and there can be less consumer product choice.

EU policy seeks to ensure that trade between member states is based on free and fair competition.

- **Article 81** prohibits agreements between firms which might prevent, restrict or distort trade, for example through price-fixing agreements.
- **Article 82** stops a firm abusing its dominant market position, e.g. by using predatory pricing (see page 114) or limiting production.

The use of **subsidies** by member states for their industries is also controlled by the EU. The purpose is to prevent competition and free trade becoming distorted, and individual government's subsidies may be disallowed.

Control of monopolies and mergers

The EU's **Merger Control Regulation** (1990) prohibits mergers that lead to or strengthen dominant market position or impede competition within the EU.

Mergers not 'caught' by the EU Articles and regulations remain subject to national competition law. In the UK, the government regulates privatised companies, e.g. through Oftel (BT) and Ofgas (British Gas), and the **Competition Commission** investigates mergers: set up by the 1998 Competition Act, its role is to investigate and make reports, and to hear appeals against decisions.

For example, in 1999 the Director-General of Fair Trading announced the referral of the grocery industry to the Commission, and the Commission started publishing its findings on the prices charged by car manufacturers.

Monopolies, mergers and restrictive trade practices fall under the 1973 **Fair Trading Act** and are referred to the Competition Commission by the Director-General of Fair Trading or the relevant Secretary of State. Anti-competitive practices fall under the 1980 **Competition Act** and are normally referred by the Director-General.

> **KEY POINT**
>
> Free and fair competition is a fundamental EU and UK policy, to ensure control of prices and choice of products.

Progress check

1 What effect does consumer protection law have on firms?
2 Why does the UK legislate against anti-competitive practices?

2 In the public interest to stop consumers being exploited, e.g. by monopoly practices.

1 Increased costs; increased awareness of customer needs; protection against unfair practices by competitors.

4.4 Other influences

After studying this section you should be able to:

- outline how firms are affected by social influences
- comment on the relevance of technological development to firms

LEARNING SUMMARY

Social influences

AQA	M3
EDEXCEL	M1
OCR	M1
WJEC	M1
NICCEA	M1

The Body Shop's reputation and image has been largely created through its ethical business stance (see page 39), and is strongly reflected in its advertising and publicity.

Modern-day organisations are aware of the importance of their **image**, and of the relationships they have with the wider community. They acknowledge their **social responsibilities** to employees, customers, shareholders and other stakeholders. Examples of specific social responsibilities include:

- **equal opportunities** – as well as obeying legislation (see page 68), firms will wish to publicise their commitment to EO
- **ethical trading** – firms have to balance moral and ethical stances with the need to make an adequate return on investment (i.e. adequate profit)
- **environmental awareness** – firms realise the negative effect of bad publicity
- **health and safety** – most firms do not limit themselves to the minimum legal requirements (see page 98), believing that a good health and safety record helps create a positive image which can be used to develop their business.

These extracts from Marks & Spencer plc's 1999 annual review illustrate how social responsibility can operate effectively and also bring commercial benefits.

> **Equal opportunities** Both our employees and our customers reflect the diversity of the communities served by Marks & Spencer. We therefore extend our commitment to equal opportunities beyond our employment practices to the ways we welcome customers to our stores. New training is helping staff to understand the specific needs of people from ethnic minority groups or those with disabilities. This also supports our commercial objective of responding to every group within the complex modern marketplace.
>
> **Health and Safety** Our investment in training many of our store safety officers towards an NVQ in health and safety is paying off for staff and organisation alike. Overall safety standards have risen even higher, meaning less time and money is lost through accident or ill health. We are also partnering public authorities in agreeing common safety standards for our buildings. This too brings business benefits, by speeding up local planning procedures for our widely located property base.
>
> **Ethical trading** Agreeing good working standards has always been important to our partnership with suppliers. This presents more of a challenge now that our global supply base has become so vast and complex. But we are determined to do what we can. So we have joined the Ethical Trading Initiative and are enforcing a set of Global Sourcing Principles. These cover areas such as workforce rights, accurate labelling of country of origin and environmental responsibility.
>
> **Environmental advance** Each year we become more sophisticated in minimising the environmental impact of our operations. During 1998 we were the first UK retailer to test an advanced software system called "Greencode". Managers at our Leicester store used this system to co-ordinate the building's heating, lighting, transport, waste disposal and other activities to cut waste and minimise its overall impact on the surrounding environment. This trial is enabling us to consider implementing this system more widely across our stores.

Firms are also influenced by **demographic trends**. Chapter 1 showed changes in family structure (see figure 1.7) and in the number of women workers: Chapter 6 (see pages 99–100) outlines issues of equality and trends in women working and equal pay. These influence a firm's recruitment and training policies (and thus its costs), and link to how it deals with equal opportunity and related issues.

Pressure groups

> **Sector** groups (e.g. British Medical Association represent a particular section; **cause** groups (e.g. ASH – Action on Smoking and Health) promote a particular cause.

These are organised groups of people with similar interests, who attempt to influence others, notably government and industries. They range in size from international organisations such as Greenpeace and Amnesty International, to small community groups concerned only with local matters.

Pressure groups affect firms: for example, trade unions act on behalf of their members, and the AA and RAC influence vehicle manufacturers on issues such as safety and fuel economy. The media also influences firms, e.g. through TV 'campaign' programmes such as 'Watchdog', affecting costs (e.g. by having to correct faulty product lines) and sales (through good or bad publicity).

A pressure group's success largely depends on the level of financial, public and political support, as well as on the organisational ability of the group itself.

Technological influences

AQA	M3
EDEXCEL	M1
OCR	M1
WJEC	M1
NICCEA	M1

Certain industries have been revolutionised by technological advances: examples include the financial sector's use of electronic funds transfer (EFT), telephone banking and e-banking, and manufacturers using CAD/CAM equipment (see page 125). Many high-street firms now offer **internet-based shopping**: in 1999, Altavista reported that 5% of world-wide internet sales took place in the UK. For business, this 'e-commerce' gives 24-hour access, allows customers in other countries access to the firm's products, and can cut costs substantially. An EU Directive which creates a consistent legal framework for e-commerce from 2000 should reinforce this growth.

> Reasons for the relatively slow take-up in the small firm sector include the cost of telephone line access and a lack of knowledge of the threat posed by not having a website.

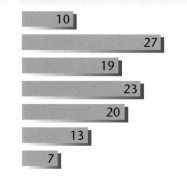

All businesses using a website % / **Micro-business (1–9 people)%**

	All businesses using a website %	Micro-business (1–9 people)%
UK	51	10
US	54	27
Canada	54	19
Germany	50	23
Japan	48	20
Italy	30	13
France	25	7

Figure 4.6 *All businesses using a website*   Source: *e-commerce@its.best.co.uk 1999*

> Benefits to firms from technological developments include lower costs, greater speed of production and sale, and improved customer satisfaction.
>
> **KEY POINT**

Progress check

1 Illustrate how a firm's ethical policy may clash with its need to make profits.

1 An ethical policy not to trade with a country because of its human rights record will affect sales and therefore profits.

Sample question and model answer

1

(a) Describe **two** types of ethical policy that might be adopted by a large do-it-yourself retailer such as 'Do-It-All' or 'B&Q', stating the reasons why they might adopt such policies. [6]

(b) Evaluate the costs and benefits of one of these policies to the stakeholders of such a company. [4]

The question is 'two in one': you need to select policies that you can explain AND give a clear justification for.

(a) A firm's ethical policy (or code) sets out how its employees respond to ethical issues: for example, issues to do with social responsibility and environmental awareness. A large do-it-yourself retailer employs many staff, and sells (and buys from suppliers) a variety of products.

If you select environmental issues, make sure that your answer focuses on business-relevant aspects of such a policy.

The first policy for such an organisation could be to consider the effects of its activities on the environment. Examples of how the company could do this include: encouraging customers to re-use plastic bags; selling environmentally-friendly and repeat-use products wherever possible; not trading with firms held to be exploiting their local environment (or the environment in general). The firm would normally draw up an environmental policy and include statements such as 'plant a new tree for every one cut down by its suppliers'. The main business reason for adopting such a policy is that increased environmental awareness on the part of buyers makes it almost compulsory in order to compete for positive publicity and to market the company effectively. (We should also acknowledge that the world's resources are finite and therefore need conserving.)

Again, focus on business-related factors.

The second policy could be to support equal opportunity (EO) issues. The company would have a stated EO policy, and comply with relevant EO legislation such as that on equal pay and on sexual/racial discrimination. By adopting such a policy, the company would (as a side-effect) gain positive publicity. Equally important is that existing staff morale is heightened by the promise and action of 'fairness': this will improve motivation and is therefore good business practice.

Again, you can start with a brief description of the key term 'stakeholders', but relate them to the type of company.

(b) Stakeholders are groups with a particular interest in the work of an organisation. The stakeholders for a large DIY retailer include employees, customers and shareholders. Concentrating on EO issues, the company's enhanced reputation and goodwill will lead to positive publicity, with resulting higher sales and higher profits. Staff morale, mentioned in (a), will also improve, with employees having an increased sense of worth, and customers and suppliers will be prepared to deal with the company. There are specific costs from such a policy: for example, monitoring and applying EO legislation, and ensuring equality of pay, have financial costs: these may have to be passed on in higher prices, making the firm less competitive and lowering its share price.

Practice examination questions

1 The British government has encouraged foreign-owned car manufacturers, such as Toyota, to set up manufacturing plants in the UK. It has at the same time provided support for other car manufacturers already based in the UK, such as Ford and Vauxhall.

   (a) What objectives might the government have in providing financial and other support to encourage Ford and Vauxhall to remain in the UK, and Toyota to establish a UK base? [10]

   (b) What are the main environmental influences affecting the way in which car manufacturers such as Toyota, Ford and Vauxhall operate? [10]

2 "There is no escape from legislation: not even when running a business. In fact, laws concerned with consumer protection have a negative effect on United Kingdom businesses."

   To what extent do you agree with this comment? [6]

3 A local town council has sought to introduce a policy banning the movement of heavy lorries through its town, by forcing non-local traffic to use another, longer local route.

   (a) What reasons might the council have for trying to establish this policy? [4]

   (b) What arguments might transport firms use against the introduction of this policy? [4]

4 "Whilst information and communications technology can lead to business efficiency in the long term, in the shorter term it can create more problems than it solves."

   Explain this statement. [6]

Chapter 5

Accounting and finance

The following topics are covered in this chapter:

- The nature and purpose of accounting
- Financial accounting
- Sources of finance
- Budgeting and forecasting

5.1 The nature and purpose of accounting

After studying this section you should be able to:

- explain the role of financial and management accounting
- identify the main users and sources of financial information

LEARNING SUMMARY

The roles of the accounting function

AQA	M1
EDEXCEL	M3
OCR	M2, M3
WJEC	M3
NICCEA	M2

Managers require **information** in order to make sound financial judgements. Management accounting contributes some of this information. It draws upon financial accounts (e.g. the final accounts and their ratios), and uses its own techniques of budgeting, costing and investment appraisal.

Financial accounting involves:

- collecting and recording information
- analysing this information
- presenting it to management
- evaluating different sources of finance

Management accounting involves:

- setting and controlling budgets
- forecasting and controlling cashflow
- classifying and calculating costs
- making investment decisions

Users of financial information

Figure 5.1 shows that these users may be **internal** or **external** to the firm.

Note the similarity between these users and the stakeholders shown on page 42.

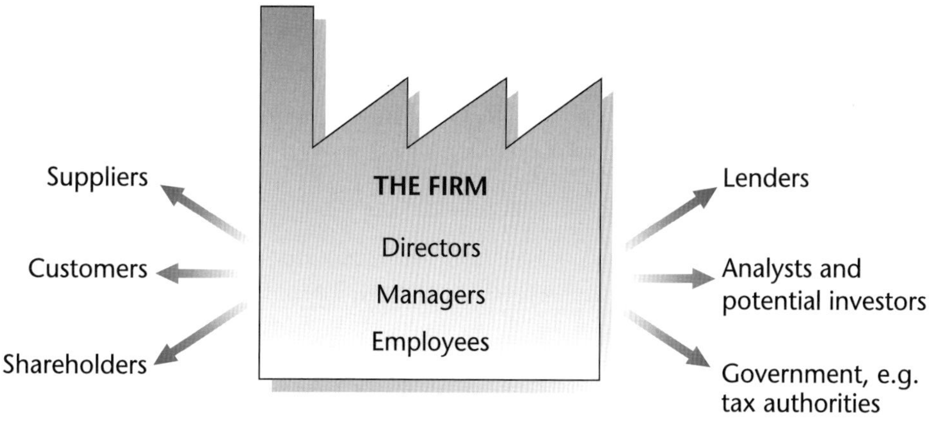

Suppliers

Customers

Shareholders

THE FIRM

Directors

Managers

Employees

Lenders

Analysts and potential investors

Government, e.g. tax authorities

Figure 5.1 Internal and external users of accounting information

Financial information deals with **external influences** on the firm – notably debtors, creditors, lenders and shareholders. Management accounting supplies an **internal analysis** of the firm's operations.

KEY POINT

5.2 Financial accounting

After studying this section you should be able to:

- *describe the different types of account*
- *state the difference between capital and revenue expenditure*
- *explain the causes, and calculate the amount, of depreciation*
- *calculate key liquidity and profitability ratios*

LEARNING SUMMARY

Types of accounts

AQA	M1
EDEXCEL	M3
OCR	M2, M3
WJEC	M3
NICCEA	M2

Capital (and profit) is a liability because of the **business entity** concept, which requires that the financial affairs of the owner(s) are kept separate from those of business. The capital and profit are **owed** (a liability) to the owner(s).

Assets

These accounts record details of the **items owned** by a firm. **Fixed assets** are long-lasting assets such as premises and machinery, which are used indirectly to make profit and which depreciate. **Current assets** – e.g. stocks, debtors and cash – fluctuate regularly and are used directly to make profit.

Liabilities

These accounts record details of **amounts owing** by a firm. The **capital** account shows the value invested by the owner(s): it is a liability because it is owed by the business to the owner or owners. **Long-term liabilities** are debts such as debentures not due to be repaid for at least one financial year. **Reserves** are also long-term liabilities of limited companies. **Current liabilities** are repayable within one year, and fluctuate regularly in value (e.g. bank overdraft, creditors – suppliers of goods on credit).

Expenses

Expense accounts record costs incurred by the firm. Examples include rent, salaries and wages, advertising, insurance, and cost of stationery.

Income

Also known as 'revenue', these accounts record the results of the firm's trading. The sales account is the main income account.

> Assets and liabilities are shown in the firm's balance sheet. Income (revenue) and expenses are shown in the firm's profit and loss account.
>
> **KEY POINT**

Final accounts

AQA	M1
EDEXCEL	M3
OCR	M2, M3
WJEC	M3
NICCEA	M2

Strictly speaking, the balance sheet is **not** an account, just a **financial statement**.

The term 'final accounts' refers to the firm's trading and profit and loss account and its balance sheet. These final accounts have important differences.

	Trading and profit and loss accounts	**Balance sheet**
Purpose	to act as an income statement and to calculate net profit	to summarise the firm's financial position
Information base	expense and revenue accounts (revenue expenditure)	asset and liability accounts (capital expenditure)
Heading	'for the period ending ...' (profit is made over a period of time)	'as at ...' (the financial position at a given point in time)

Figure 5.2 *Final accounts*

The trading account

Its purpose is to calculate **gross profit**, by deducting the firm's cost of sales from its sales income. Its basic construction is shown in Figure 5.3.

N. Merchant Trading account for year ending 31 December	£ (000)	£ (000)
Sales		400
Less cost of sales:		
Opening stock	55	
Purchases	290	
	345	
Closing stock	(45)	
Gross profit		300
		100

Figure 5.3 *Trading account*

The profit and loss account

Its purpose is to calculate **net profit**, which is the excess of the firm's gross profit (plus any other revenues, such as rent receivable from sub-letting premises) over its expenses. Figure 5.4 illustrates a typical profit and loss account.

N. Merchant Profit and loss account for year ending 31 December	£ (000)	£ (000)
Gross profit		100
Less expenses:		
Administration	32	
Selling and distribution	16	
Financial	12	
Net profit		60
		40

Figure 5.4 *Profit and loss account*

The profit may have to be **appropriated** (shared out). Partnership appropriation of profits may be influenced by:

- the amount of capital invested by each partner
- the amount of work each partner does in the partnership.

A limited company's net profit presents the directors with the same decision that people have to make regarding their own income – how much to **spend** and how much to **save**. The 'spending' element consists of compulsory spending on corporation tax, and voluntary spending through distributing share dividends. The higher the dividend, the more content shareholders will be: but more cash must be paid out, which puts pressure on the company's cash resources. The 'saving' element occurs where the directors decide to hold back some of the net profit (and by doing so, preserve cash) in the form of **reserves**.

The balance sheet

Its purpose is to show the firm's **financial position at a stated point in time**. It lists assets and liabilities under their group headings.

Modern balance sheet layouts show the firm's **net current assets**, often called 'working capital'. Working capital is the difference between current assets and current liabilities, and is one of the most important figures for a business because it indicates **liquidity**, the ability of the business to repay its debts as these debts become due for payment.

<table>
<tr><td colspan="2">Working Capital = Current Assets minus Current Liabilities</td><td rowspan="3" style="text-align:center">KEY POINT</td></tr>
<tr><td>Current assets</td><td>cash and 'near-cash' (e.g. amounts owed by debtors which will shortly be paid)</td></tr>
<tr><td>Current liabilities</td><td>short-term debts owed, which will soon have to be paid by the firm</td></tr>
</table>

N. Merchant Balance sheet as at 31 December

	£ (000) Cost	£ (000) Depreciation	£ (000) Net
Fixed assets			
Land and buildings	100	–	100
Plant and equipment	24	6	18
Vehicles	5	3	2
	129	9	120
Current assets			
Stocks		45	
Debtors		25	
Bank and cash		20	
		90	
Current liabilities			
Creditors	20		
Accrued expenses	10		
Net current assets		30	
Net assets			60
			180
Capital			
Opening balance			140
Net profit for year			40
			180

Figure 5.5 Balance sheet

Capital and revenue expenditure in final accounts

Asset and expense accounts record purchases made by a business. These purchases are analysed under two headings.

Capital expenditure	Revenue expenditure
the firm buys new (or improves existing) fixed assets	the firm pays its everyday running expenses
e.g. buy a new delivery van	*e.g. pays rent, pays wages*
shown in the Balance Sheet	shown in the Profit and Loss account

<table>
<tr><td>Capital expenditure does not affect profit calculation, but revenue expenditure does. If we wrongly classify capital expenditure as revenue expenditure, or vice versa, the profit figure will be incorrect.</td><td style="text-align:center">KEY POINT</td></tr>
</table>

Depreciation in final accounts

Fixed assets **depreciate** (fall in value) each year. An estimated annual charge – the depreciation provision – is made against profits so that each year's profit bears its share of the total cost of depreciation. If this was not done, one year's profit – the profit for the year in which the fixed asset was sold – would bear the full cost, and comparisons between it and other years' profits would be unfair. The annual depreciation provision is charged against (gross) profit, and total depreciation is deducted from the fixed asset value in the balance sheet.

Depreciation of fixed assets can be caused by:

- wear and tear – everyday use (e.g. a vehicle) will gradually wear out that asset
- obsolescence – the asset (e.g. a computer) becomes out-of-date
- depletion – the fixed asset is used up, e.g. extraction of minerals from a mine.

There are two popular methods used to calculate depreciation.

> Depreciation is an example of a **provision**. This is created when a firm has expenses but the exact amount of the expenses is not known with any certainty.

1 Straight line (equal instalment) method

$$\frac{\text{original cost} - \text{residual (resale) value}}{\text{estimated life}}$$

This allocates the estimated depreciation cost equally to each year of the fixed asset's life. For example, a vehicle costing £16,000 with an estimated life of five years and resale value of £6,000 has an annual depreciation of £2,000 (£16,000 – £6,000 = £10,000, divided by 5).

2 Reducing (Diminishing) Balance method

> a fixed percentage is applied each year to the written-down value of the fixed asset

This allocates greater amounts for depreciation to the earlier years of the fixed asset (which often more realistically reflects the true value of the asset). If the above vehicle was depreciated by this method, using a 25% figure:

year 1 = £4,000 depreciation, leaving £12,000 net book value (NBV)
year 2 = £3,000 depreciation, leaving £9,000 NBV
year 3 = £2,250 depreciation, leaving £6,750 NBV (etc.)

> Depreciation illustrates the **accrual** (or 'matching') concept, where income and expenses are matched against the period to which they refer.

Progress check

1 What is the purpose of
(a) a profit and loss account;
(b) a balance sheet?

2 A business buys a fixed asset for £400,000. How much will this asset be depreciated by in year 2, using
(a) the straight line method (it has a useful life of four years and a residual value of £80,000);
(b) the reducing balance method (an annual rate of 20% is to be applied)?

1 (a) Historical statement of revenue and expenses, showing net profit; (b) historical statement of what a firm owns (assets) and what it owes (liabilities).
2 (a) £400.00 – £80,000 = £320,000 divided by 4 = £80,000
(b) Year 1 = 20% of £400,000 = £80,000; year 2 = 20% of £320,000 = £64,000

Accounting ratios

AQA	A2
EDEXCEL	M1
OCR	A2
WJEC	A2
NICCEA	A2

The firm's final accounts are interpreted by calculating ratios. The results are then used to compare the current performance of the firm against:

* that of its **competitors**, to establish its relative competitiveness
* its **own performance** in previous years, to identify any trends.

Interested groups

Group	Interest	Main reason for interest
Managers	liquidity profitability asset efficiency investment	Re-election of directors; share dividend levels; financial reward; survival of the firm
Employees	liquidity profitability	Job prospects; pay claims; reward (e.g. if in profit-sharing scheme)
Lenders	liquidity	Assess the firm's ability to meet their debts
Investors	liquidity profitability asset efficiency investment	(Short term) dividends and share values; (long term) share values; security of investment
Government	liquidity profitability	income from taxation; meeting economic objectives (e.g. full employment)

Profitability ratios

Profitability measures a firm's **total profit compared to the resources used** in making that profit.

> This return can be compared with other investments to see whether it is worth staying in business.

1 Return on capital employed (ROCE)

$$\frac{\text{net profit}}{\text{capital employed}} \times 100$$

This shows the profitability of the investment by calculating its percentage return.

> The NP margin will fall if the GP margin has also fallen, or if the firm's other expenses as a percentage of sales has risen.

2 Net profit margin (NP ratio, or NP %)

$$\frac{\text{net profit}}{\text{sales}} \times 100$$

This shows the percentage of turnover – sales – represented by net profit, i.e. how many pence out of every £1 sold is net profit.

3 Gross profit margin (GP ratio, or GP %)

$$\frac{\text{gross profit}}{\text{sales}} \times 100$$

This indicates the percentage of turnover represented by gross profit.

Liquidity ratios

> The firm's ability to survive can also partly be judged from its **capital gearing** (see page 81).

These ratios help the firm estimate whether it is **overtrading**. This occurs when a firm is successful and expands without sufficient long-term capital, putting pressure on its working capital.

1 Working capital (current) ratio

current assets (CA) : current liabilities (CL)

If current liabilities exceed current assets, the firm may have difficulty in meeting its debts. Extra short-term borrowing, to pay off creditors, costs the firm money (interest). If the firm sells assets to help meet its debts, it risks loss of production and future expansion. Too high a level of working capital may also exist, indicating that the firm is not using its liquid assets productively (e.g. they are 'tied up' in surplus stocks).

2 Liquid ratio ('acid test' or 'quick assets')

CA – stock : CL

> This is a more cautious assessment than the current ratio.

Using this ratio lets us see whether the firm can meet short-term debts without having to sell stock (which is regarded as the least liquid current asset).

3 Debtors' collection period ('Debtor days')

$$\frac{\text{debtors} \times 365}{\text{sales}}$$

> This ratio measures how efficient the firm is at collecting its debts.

This shows the time (average days) that it takes debtors to pay the firm.

4 Creditors' collection period ('Creditor days')

$$\frac{\text{creditors} \times 365}{\text{purchases}}$$

This calculates the average length of credit the firm receives from its suppliers.

> **Liquidity**, associated with cashflow, measures the firm's ability to survive in the short run. **Profitability** is a clearer indicator of its ability to survive in the longer term.
>
> **KEY POINT**

Asset efficiency ratios

1 Rate of stock turnover ('Stockturn')

$$\frac{\text{cost of sales}}{\text{average stock}} \quad \text{(stated as '...times per period')}$$

> If the stockturn figure is falling, the firm is taking longer to sell stock: reasons include keeping higher stock levels, or falling demand for its products.

The purpose is to calculate how frequently the firm sells its stock.

2 Asset turnover

$$\frac{\text{sales}}{\text{net assets}}$$

This assesses the value of sales generated by the net assets (which represent the capital being employed in the firm).

3 Gearing

$$\frac{\text{prior charge capital}}{\text{total long-term capital}} \quad \text{(long-term loans + preference shares)}$$

> Higher gearing is often found in larger companies, and can vary from country to country (e.g. Japanese companies tend to be more highly geared than UK ones).

This analyses the different types of payments made to capital. Companies with more than 50% prior charge capital are called 'high-geared': those with less than 50% are 'low-geared'. Gearing is important when additional capital is required. If a company is already highly geared, it may find it difficult to take out further loans. The advantages of high gearing are similar to those associated with loan, rather than share, capital (page 83).

Progress check

1 Calculate these ratios for N. Merchant (see Figures 5.3, 5.4 and 5.5): (a) ROCE; (b) net profit margin; (c) gross profit margin; (d) current ratio; (e) liquid ratio; (f) debtor days; (g) creditor days; (h) stockturn.

2 A company's annual sales are £16.5 million and cost of goods is £11 million. Average stock is £550,000. Calculate the stock turnover ratio.

2 Twenty times per annum = once every 18 days.

1 (a) 28.6% (£140,000 capital employed generates £40,000 net profit): (b) 10% (£40,000 as % of £400,000);
(c) 25% (£100,000 as % of £400,000); (d) 3 : 1 (90 : 30); (e) 1.5 : 1 (45 : 30); (f) (25 × 365)/400 = 22.8 days;
(g) (20 × 365)/290 = 25.2 days; (h) 300/50 = six times a year (once every two months).

81

5.3 Sources of finance

After studying this section you should be able to:

- describe suitable long-, medium- and short-term sources of finance
- suggest an appropriate source of finance in a given situation

Internal sources

AQA	M1
EDEXCEL	M3
OCR	M2, M3
WJEC	M3
NICCEA	M2

> The finance available is determined by the **ownership** and **size** of the firm.

Retained profits

Private sector firms can preserve cash through retaining profits, e.g. where a limited company decides to move profit to reserves (page 76) rather than to distribute it as cash (share dividends). This is the main internal source of funds for many firms, although the source depends on the level of profits.

Control of working capital and cashflow

Extending the average credit it takes from suppliers, and/or reducing the average credit period it allows its customers, will improve the firm's cashflow; ratios to calculate debtor and creditor days (page 81) are relevant here. Other controls include reducing stock levels (see stockturn ratio, page 81) and postponing the payment of **expense creditors** (e.g. electricity bill), to preserve cash.

> The firm's operating cycle describes the link between cash movements and working capital. It provides a clear indication to the accountant of how the firm's production cycle, and credit periods allowed and taken, affect cashflow.

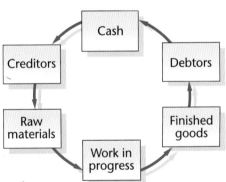

Figure 5.6 The operating cycle

Sale of assets

A firm may have surplus assets, e.g. during an economic recession or internal rationalisation. These assets can be sold to raise finance. The firm may also sell an asset to a buyer, then lease it back over a period of time: known as **sale and leaseback**, funds are generated for the firm, and it still has use of the asset.

External sources

AQA	M1
EDEXCEL	M3
OCR	M2, M3
WJEC	M3
NICCEA	M2

Family and friends

Associated with the sole trader and partnership forms of business organisation, family and friends can provide low-cost finance, usually with little if any security being required. The amount of finance available in this form is often quite small.

Share issues

A limited company normally obtains most of its permanent capital by issuing ordinary and/or preference shares. Its **authorised** capital (the maximum that can be issued) is contained in its **memorandum of association** (page 38).

Ordinary shares (equity) receive a variable dividend, which relies on surplus profits after all other payments: they may receive high dividends in times of high profits, and no dividend when profits are low.

Preference shares have a fixed dividend and do not carry a vote, so – unlike ordinary shares – their issue does not affect the control of a company.

Group		1998		1997	
		Shares	**$ million**	**Shares**	**$ million**
Non-equity	8% (now 5.6% + tax credit) cumulative first preference shares of £1 each	7,232,838	12	7,232,838	12
	9% (now 6.3% + tax credit) cumulative second preference shares of £1 each	5,473,414	9	5,473,414	9
Equity	Ordinary shares of 50 pence each	9,683,010,023	4842	3,835,209,036	1,918
	Ordinary shares of 25 pence each	–	–	5,762,583,600	2,391
			4863		4,330

Figure 5.7 Share capital, BP Amoco plc, 1998

Unlike dividends, however, the interest payments must always be met. Failure to do so may lead to closure of the firm.

The term 'debenture' refers to the issued document outlining the nature of the loan.

Other long-term finance (normally five years and over)

Using long-term loans for finance brings certain benefits:

- interest payments may be eroded by inflation
- these payments are made out of gross profit (untaxed income), whereas dividend payments come out of (taxed) net profit
- the lender has no direct say in the running of the firm.

Debentures may be secured against specific assets, or assets in general: the lender recovers the asset if the borrower fails to make interest payments.

Medium-term finance (between one and five years)

Bank and other loans are fixed sums agreed between the borrower and lender, for a fixed term. Unlike overdrafts, a special account is opened, interest being charged on the full balance. Security is required by the lender.

With leasing, the firm obtains equipment without having to buy (own) it.

- A large capital outlay is therefore avoided by the lessee (hirer).
- Payments are regular, known in advance, and made out of taxable income.
- Income generated from using the asset can contribute towards payment.
- No specific security is normally required.
- Over time, the asset can be upgraded or the agreement ended.

But the lessee continues to pay for an item that will never be owned.

However, the amount paid on credit will far exceed the original purchase price.

Hire purchase and credit sale agreements allow the buyer to acquire the asset immediately, and pay for it over time. The asset is owned – on the first payment with a credit sale, on the final payment with HP – and the cost is spread.

Short-term sources of finance (less than one year)

Although usually less expensive and more flexible than loans, an overdraft facility can easily be withdrawn by the lender.

Overdrafts are agreed with a bank, letting the firm overdraw on its account up to an agreed maximum, with a charge based on the amount overdrawn.

Factoring occurs when a firm sells trade debts at below face value to a factoring agent in return for immediate cash. The firm loses some of the value of the debt, offset by the quick receipt of cash which can be used immediately.

Progress check

1 State the difference between leasing and credit sale.

2 Give **three** differences between shares and debentures.

2 Share dividend, debenture interest; share owner, debenture lender; share dividend paid from net profit, debenture interest from gross profit.

1 Leasing, asset is never owned; credit sale, owned after first payment.

5.4 Budgeting and forecasting

After studying this section you should be able to:

- *explain how variance analysis leads to management by exception*
- *describe the purpose and difficulty of cash forecasting*
- *apply your knowledge of cost classification to calculate and show break-even*

LEARNING SUMMARY

Budgeting

AQA	M1
EDEXCEL	M3
OCR	M2, M3
WJEC	M3
NICCEA	M2

A budget is **a plan expressed in money**, which relates to a **defined time period**. Budgets allow a firm's activities to be:

- **co-ordinated**: through the master budget, which brings together the different functions of the firm, ensuring managers plan and work together
- **controlled**: by comparing actual performance with budgeted performance, the level of individual and departmental spending is reviewed, and individual managers take responsibility for meeting targets
- **communicated**: through involving all staff in creating budgets, allowing delegation to take place and motivating staff to achieve budgeted performance.

Setting budgets

Budgets are not easy to set in practice. One problem is incomplete or inaccurate data, e.g. in estimating future sales volumes and prices. Also, budgets can be seen as a financial 'straightjacket': the temptation is to set too easy a target to achieve.

A **zero base budget** may be set: the budget is set at zero, requiring the manager to justify all expenditure. An alternative zero budget approach is where the manager uses last year's cost figures, having to present a case for an increase (e.g. due to inflation). Zero budgeting makes managers **set priorities** – the zero budget constraint makes them eliminate those activities having the lowest priority.

> In smaller businesses, budget creation is often quick and informal.

Budgeting is a formal process. **Budget committees** oversee the creation of budgets and co-ordinate the completed budgets, and a **budget manual** gives a written record of procedures and individual responsibilities.

Budgeting is subject to the **principal budget factor**: this is the item that limits the firm's activities. The most common principal budget factor is the level of demand for the products: other examples include the availability of raw materials or skilled labour, and machine capacity.

The main budgets

Budgets can be prepared for each major function or activity of the firm. Figure 5.8 summarises the main budgets, in their normal order of creation.

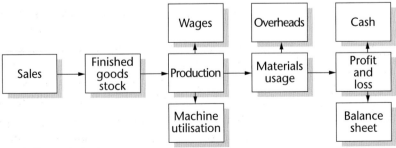

Figure 5.8 The main budgets

A budgeted profit and loss account – and, at a later stage, a budgeted balance sheet – will be prepared from a range of functional budgets, including:

Sales budget

Sales units and value are calculated on the basis of past sales, current market research, and an estimate of the competition.

Production budget

Based on the sales budget, it includes budgeted changes in stock. Budgeted production is analysed into resource requirements for materials, labour and machine operating hours.

Cash budget

This summarises anticipated cash inflows and outflows. Inflows are based on the sales budget, and other receipts are also included. Budgeted cash outflows for labour, materials and other costs are identified from other budgets. Capital expenditure is also included.

Budgetary control

Once budgets are implemented, managers can compare the expected (budgeted) performance of their department with its actual performance. Control takes place through management by exception. Management by exception is based on this comparison of expected against actual. Any difference between budgeted and actual performance produces a variance, which may be:

- favourable – e.g. where actual sales exceed budgeted, or where a particular cost comes in below budget, or
- adverse (unfavourable) – e.g. actual sales have not reached budgeted targets, or an actual cost is above its budgeted level.

For example, here is a cost and income summary for a firm:

	Budget (£)	Actual (£)
Sales income	250,000	260,000
Labour costs	80,000	85,000
Materials costs	40,000	38,000
Overheads	10,000	11,000
Profit (sales less costs)	120,000	126,000

The actual profit is £6,000 higher than the budgeted profit. The variances making up this difference are:

sales	£10,000 favourable (actual revenue higher than budget)
labour	£5,000 adverse (actual cost higher than budget)
material	£2,000 favourable (lower actual cost)
overheads	£1,000 adverse (higher actual cost)

(£12,000 total favourable less £6,000 total adverse = £6,000 overall favourable).

Some variances are due to factors controllable by an individual manager: in this example, the manager may have authorised the lower selling price in the hope that, by selling more, the product's price elasticity (page 24) will increase total revenue. Managers can only be held accountable for controllable variances. Other variances may not be under the manager's control, who is therefore not held responsible: for example, an adverse wages variance may result from an unexpected national pay rise, outside the control of anyone in the firm.

Cost and profit centres are created to support budgetary control. A cost centre is a location such as a production line, an item of equipment (e.g. a photocopier) or even a person, acting as a collecting point for costs. These costs can then be

In practice, budgets are 'flexed', i.e. adjusted for changes in volume, so that the comparison between actual and budget is based on the same figure.

analysed. A **profit centre** is similar in that it collects costs, but also collects income associated with those costs. A profit figure can then be calculated and used in budgetary control and decision-making generally.

Cash-flow forecasting

AQA	M1
EDEXCEL	M3
OCR	M2, M3
WJEC	M3
NICCEA	M2

> Credit control is an important function for any business trying to control its cash flow.

Cash flow is sometimes confused with profit: the assumption is that, if a firm makes £1 million profit after tax, it has also increased its cash and bank balance by £1 million. Large profits can be made, and yet the cash and bank balances may at the same time have fallen. Reasons include:

- cash is used to buy fixed assets (this has no great effect on the profit figure)
- sales are made on credit (no immediate cash, but profit increases)
- suppliers are paid quickly (cash falls, with no effect on profit).

The profit figure is a key element in calculating **profitability**, whereas the firm's cash flow is used to check the **liquidity** position (see page 80). Profit is often seen as being more important to the **long-term** survival of the firm, and cash flow as the key factor in **short-term** survival.

Cash-flow forecasts are therefore used. We can use these figures, adapted from a past question, to illustrate how a cash-flow forecast is prepared.

Balance sheet extracts (end of 2001): cash £60,000; debtors £150,000; creditors £160,000; tax owing £300,000. The debtors will pay in January; the creditors will be paid January (50%) and February (50%); tax will be paid in March.

Year 2002 forecast:	Jan	Feb	Mar	Apr	May	Jun
Sales £ (000)	120	600	600	400	120	120
Materials £ (000)	80	80	90	90	90	90

Other information for the first 6 months of 2002:
Sales are on one month's credit, materials on two months' credit.
Monthly overheads are £45,000, payable in the same month.
Wages are paid in cash each month: total monthly wage bill is £90,000.
New shares will be issued in February: £50,000.

1 Total receipts are calculated: debtors pay one month after the sales so, for example, December's sales figure equals January's cash received figure.

2 Total payments are calculated: half of December's creditors are paid in January and half in February, and the materials figures appear as cash payments two months later; the other payments occur in the same month.

3 The net receipt/payment of cash is calculated for each month.

	Jan	Feb	Mar	Apr	May	Jun
Receipts (£000):						
from debtors	150	120	600	600	400	120
from new share issue		50				
Total receipts	150	170	600	600	400	120
Payments (£000):						
to creditors/for materials	80	80	80	80	90	90
for overheads	45	45	45	45	45	45
for wages	90	90	90	90	90	90
for tax			300			
Total payments	215	215	515	215	225	225
Net monthly receipts/payments	(65)	(45)	85	385	175	(105)
Opening cash balance (£000)	60	(5)	(50)	35	420	595
Closing cash balance (£000)	(5)	(50)	35	420	595	490

4 The closing cash balance is calculated from how the month's opening cash balance is affected by the net receipts/payments. Brackets are used to indicate a negative balance.

In this example, the firm would have to make sure it had overdraft facilities for January and February, or another way of covering the shortfalls of cash. Also, there is a large surplus of cash later in the period, which will need investing or otherwise using efficiently on behalf of the firm.

> It is as important to identify large cash surpluses as well as large cash deficits, to ensure surplus cash is used efficiently.

The above example can also be used to illustrate the problems of cash-flow forecasting. Any forecast is likely to prove inaccurate: for example, actual sales will differ from forecast sales. The firm's directors will therefore need to **monitor the accuracy** of the cash-flow forecast, and take appropriate action.

If the forecast indicates that cashflow must be improved, the directors have a number of options. They can:

- calculate 'debtor days' and 'creditor days' **ratios** (see page 81) to assess credit periods taken and allowed
- **factor** debtors (see page 83)
- use **sale/leaseback** (see page 83)
- examine other ways of controlling **working capital** (see page 82), for example by reducing stock levels.

Progress check

1 What is the difference between budgeting and budgetary control?

2 How does cash-flow forecasting aid the survival of a firm?

2 It indicates the likely future liquidity of the firm, enabling appropriate action to be taken if a cash shortfall is expected.

1 Budgeting is the act of setting budgets; budgetary control compares budgeted and actual figures for decision-making purposes.

Cost classification and analysis

AQA	M1
EDEXCEL	M3
OCR	M2, M3
WJEC	M3
NICCEA	M2

Classifying costs allows analysis to take place. For example, break-even analysis classifies costs as fixed or variable. Classifying costs as direct or indirect is necessary for **absorption costing**, a costing method that 'absorbs' overheads into product costs: for example, factory rent (a factory overhead) must be absorbed into the cost of products made in the factory. Costs are also analysed for product pricing, stock valuation, and comparing the relative profitability of product lines.

Direct and indirect costs

> Direct materials + direct labour + direct expenses = prime cost.

- **Direct** costs are linked with particular product lines: they are therefore costs that can be identified **precisely** with a product or process.

> Indirect labour + indirect material + indirect expenses = **overheads**.

- **Indirect** costs are shared between product lines, because they do not relate to one product in particular. In practice, these costs must be apportioned to the different products.

For example, a car manufacturer has sheet steel and engine parts as direct materials, assembly-line employees as direct labour, and the cost of transporting product-specific items (such as engine parts) as direct expenses. Indirect costs for this manufacturer include supervisory wages and business rates. These costs appear in the firm's **manufacturing account**.

Fixed and variable costs

This classification is based on the way that costs behave when output changes.

- **Fixed costs** remain constant as output changes. Factory rent and business rates are two examples often given, although in practice rent is a stepped cost: as output increases, the firm may need extra space and therefore at some stage may have to pay additional rent.
- **Variable costs** change in proportion to changes in output. A popular illustration is direct materials: doubling the output typically doubles the cost of materials required. In practice, there may not be a perfect match (economies of scale lower the unit price of materials as output increases).
- **Semi-variable costs** are also found. Commonly used illustrations are power and telephone, which often include a fixed element (a standing charge, e.g. for line rental) and a variable element based on the number of units used.

Break-even analysis

AQA	M1
EDEXCEL	M3
OCR	M2, M3
WJEC	M3
NICCEA	M2

Classifying costs as either fixed or variable is required for break-even analysis. This is also particularly useful for **contribution pricing** (see page 113), and provides important information for production purposes. The break-even point can be calculated mathematically and/or displayed graphically.

Calculating the break-even point

The calculation is based on the concept of **contribution** (see also pricing decisions, page 113). Every product made has a variable cost: it also has a (higher) selling price. The difference between these two figures is known as the 'contribution' made by the individual product. This contribution is made towards the firm's fixed costs. When enough of these individual contributions have been made, the firm's total costs will be covered and it is at break-even point, making neither a profit nor a loss.

If, therefore, the firm has fixed costs totalling £6,000, variable costs of £1 per unit and a unit selling price of £2.50:

- unit contribution is £2.50 – £1.00 = £1.50
- break-even point is £6,000 / £1.50 = 4,000 units

The firm must make and sell 4,000 units to break even: every unit sold above this figure increases net profit by £1.50, and every unit that the firm fails to make and sell below 4,000 produces a loss of £1.50. At an output of 4,000 units:

total revenue = 4,000 x £2.50 = £10,000
total costs = 4,000 x £1 = £4,000 variable + £6,000 fixed = £10,000

It is easy to calculate profit or loss once the break-even point is known.

Profit = contribution x number of units **above** break-even;

Loss = contribution x number of units **below** break-even.

If the firm currently makes and sells 6,000 units, its **margin of safety** – the number of units by which production and sales can fall before it starts to make a loss – is 2,000 units. The profit at this level of production and sales is:

		£
Total revenue = 6,000 x £2.50		= 15,000
Total costs	= fixed	= (6,000)
	+ variable (6,000 x £1)	= (6,000)
Profit		= 3,000

> Since contribution above 4,000 break-even units = profit:
>
> profit = 2,000 x £1.50 = £3,000, agreeing with the full calculation shown.

Graphical display

This is shown by Figure 5.9. The sales revenue line is plotted and the total cost line is represented by the fixed cost line (parallel to the horizontal axis) plus the variable cost line. The information used above in calculating the break-even point is also used here.

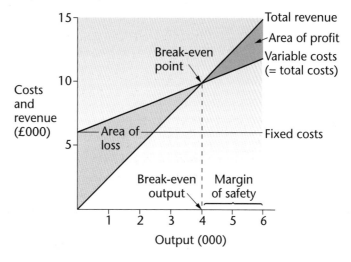

Figure 5.9 Break-even chart

Limitations of break-even analysis

- The chart only applies to a single product, or to a fixed 'mix' of products.
- Not all costs can be easily and accurately classified as fixed or variable (e.g. those semi-variable costs with a standing charge).
- Sales prices are assumed constant at all activity levels: this may be unrealistic.
- Production and sales are assumed to be the same figure.
- Fixed costs change over time and can change with volume (e.g. stepped costs: see page 88).
- Unit variable costs may change with output, due to economies or diseconomies of scale (see pages 56–7).

> Break-even analysis remains helpful to management in planning production and selling levels.

Progress check

1 Distinguish between direct and indirect costs, giving an example of each.

2 Calculate the break-even point for a firm with fixed costs of £110,000, unit variable costs of £3.45 and a selling price of £8.95.

1 Directly linked to product, e.g. materials used in manufacture; not directly linked to product, e.g. general factory cleaning materials.

2 Contribution = £8.95 – £3.45 = £5.50
Break-even point = £110,000 / £5.50 = 20,000 units
(Break-even cost/revenue figure = 20,000 x £8.95 = £179,000).

89

Sample questions and model answers

1

Explain the ways in which accounting may be of use to the managers of a company producing bottled drinks. [8]

The examiner will look for your ability to apply your general knowledge of accounting principles to a bottled drinks manufacturer.

All organisations must control their finances. The accounting function records the movement of cash and value throughout the organisation, regardless of what it makes. Through the use of standard costing and budgetary control, costs of manufacturing the drinks are identified, and prices can be set using a 'cost-plus' approach. The firm can calculate whether it is cheaper to buy in items such as bottles, or whether to make them on the premises. Credit control systems can be used by the firm to monitor its debtors, if selling on credit. Through using a management by exception approach, all controllable variances (variations) can be brought to the attention of managers. Ratio analysis of past accounts helps management to spot financial trends and key areas for action.

At some stage in your answer you need to summarise the general management features of an efficient accounting system.

An efficient accounting system enables management to plan ahead, for example through budgeting; to co-ordinate its various functions through meetings to discuss budgets; to communicate financial performance and achievement; and, by doing so, to motivate staff through involvement.

2

What factors cause cash-flow problems? Outline **two** ways in which a firm might overcome these problems. State **one** drawback associated with each. [6]

Don't limit your answer to, for example, 'increased delay of debtors repaying': follow this up with the result ('…slowing down cash receipts…').

Reasons for cashflow problems include: increased delay of debtors repaying, thereby slowing down cash receipts and reducing liquidity; creditors are being paid earlier than before or earlier than necessary, reducing cash levels; more cash than necessary is tied up in stocks.

Other areas you could mention include borrowing, improved budgetary control, sale/leaseback, and disposal of surplus assets.

A firm might decide to factor its debts. This produces quick cash, but the firm does not receive the full debt, the factor charging for the service. The firm might also try to use trade (suppliers') credit to a greater extent, lengthening the credit period taken from suppliers: the drawback is that this might affect trading conditions, e.g. withdrawal of credit by supplier, and affect the firm's reputation.

Practice examination questions

1 (a) Courtmills Ltd makes sports clothing. One product line is sports sweaters which it sells to retailers at £20 each. The firm's projected output is 80,000 units a year although it has the capacity to make 100,000. The figures below show the relevant costs for the sweaters.

Overhead costs   £300,000
Labour cost/unit   £2
Material cost/unit   £8
Other variable costs £2

Showing your working in full calculate:

(i)   the contribution of each sweater sold [2]

(ii) the break-even level of output in respect of quantity and revenue [4]

(iii) the margin of safety at the proposed level of output [2]

(iv) the standard cost of each sweater at the proposed level of output. [4]

(b) Courtmills Ltd has been approached by a high street retail chain with an order for 20,000 sweaters at £13 each. The sweaters would be produced under an own brand label and would require the purchase of a new machine costing £20,000.

Assessing the numerical and non-numerical factors together, what advice would you give to Courtmills Limited in accepting or rejecting the order? [20]

(c) Below is an extract from the profit and loss account and balance sheet of Courtmills Ltd for 1998. Some items have not been calculated yet.

	£million		£million
Sales revenue	1.4	Fixed assets	2.5
Cost of sales	0.58	Current assets	0.7
Gross profit		Less current liabilities	0.3
Less expenses	0.65	Net assets	
Net profit		Long term liabilities	1.6
		Shareholders' funds	1.3
		Capital employed	

Showing your workings in full, calculate the:

(i)   gross profit margin; [2]

(ii) net profit margin; [2]

(iii) return on capital employed. [2]

(d) Calculate and comment on the firm's:

(i)   current ratio; [4]

(ii) gearing ratio. [4]

2 (a) Hilights Ltd makes soft toys for a number of chain stores. The most expensive pieces of production equipment are the two cutting and sewing machines that are computer aided. Each machine costs £70,000 and is expected to have a working life of five years. The company accountant expects to sell the machines at the end of their useful lives for about £3,500 each.

Assess how the use of an alternative method of depreciation would affect the company's reported profits. [12]

(b) In August the company accountant prepares a cash-flow forecast. Most sales are on credit terms. The chart below shows a summary of the cash flow for Hilights Ltd.

Month	Sept £000	Oct £000	Nov £000	Dec £000	Jan £000	Feb £000	Mar £000	Apr £000
Opening Balance	10	(21)	(96)	(252)	(335)			
Sales receipts	18	15	37	92	225	178	24	20
Expenses								
Purchases	14	20	45	50	8	8	8	10
Wages	15	45	120	90	17	12	18	17
Overheads	20	25	28	35	25	20	20	20
Balance	(21)	(96)	(252)	(335)				

(i) Use the information above to calculate the projected cash balance of Hilights Limited at the end of January and February. [2]

(ii) Evaluate the ways in which a business such as Hilights Limited could overcome its cash-flow problems. [10]

Edexcel Specimen Unit 3 Qs 1 and 2

Chapter 6

Human resource management

The following topics are covered in this chapter:

- Human resource planning
- Recruitment, selection and training
- Legislation and work
- Motivation

6.1 Human resource planning

After studying this section you should be able to:

LEARNING SUMMARY

- outline the key areas of responsibility of the HRM function
- describe key influences on an organisation's workforce planning
- explain how labour force trends can affect a firm's operation

HRM functions

AQA	M2
EDEXCEL	M1
OCR	M2, M3
WJEC	M4
NICCEA	M2

The **Human Resource Management** (HRM) (Personnel) function exists in all organisations, either as one of the roles of a general manager in a small firm, or as a separate department in a large company. The key areas of HRM are:

Area	Reasons
Manpower planning	To identify and meet labour shortfalls; to review employees' current skills; to help employees achieve their potential.
Recruitment and selection	To ensure organisational objectives are met; to bring in new ideas; to appoint suitably qualified and skilled employees.
Training and development	To allow new employees to settle in quickly; to help employees develop and contribute more to the work of the organisation.
Appraisal	To encourage employees to achieve their potential; to support employees in their attempts to achieve personal goals.
Welfare	To help employees satisfy their personal needs.
Consultation and negotiation	To communicate key policies; to motivate employees through involvement; to anticipate and identify employee concerns.

Workforce planning

AQA	M2
EDEXCEL	M1
OCR	M2, M3
WJEC	M4
NICCEA	M2

Workforce planning seeks to ensure that:

- corporate plan workforce requirements are identified and implemented
- workforce levels guarantee production can take place
- workforce quality leads to improved productivity
- controllable workforce costs meet budget targets.

> **KEY POINT**
>
> The key function of HRM is to ensure there will be the **right number** of employees, of the **right quality**, in the **right place** at the **right time**.

Labour turnover

An important source of information for, and influence on, the workforce plan is the level of the firm's labour turnover (LTO). LTO can benefit a firm by introducing new staff with new ideas, although high LTO may indicate:

- low morale amongst the employees

- pay levels that are below comparable local rates
- high costs of recruitment and training
- lower production.

> **Retention profiles** showing staff according to the year they joined the organisation, can be constructed and analysed.

$$LTO = \frac{\text{Number of leavers in the year*}}{\text{Average number employed in the year}} \times 100$$

(*this figure is adjusted to take account of unavoidable reasons for leaving)

Influences on the plan

Workforce planning requires managers to assess staffing needs for a number of years ahead. These plans are often based on a **STEP** analysis of the external influences on the organisation:

- **Social** influences – e.g. increased numbers of women wanting to return to work
- **Technological** influences – e.g. new production processes requiring new skills
- **Economic** influences – e.g. free movement of labour in the EU
- **Political** influences – e.g. government training schemes.

A firm's workforce strategy is influenced by supply and demand.

If the labour supply exceeds the firm's demand for labour:	**If the firm's demand for labour exceeds its supply:**
• voluntary or compulsory redundancy • redeployment and retraining • encouraging early retirement • encouraging 'natural wastage'	• additional advertising • retraining programmes • acknowledging labour as a limiting factor in forecasting • better labour market competitiveness (e.g. through increased pay rates)

Demographic factors

Some key trends in the labour market have been indicated in Chapter 1 (see pages 19 and 20). Other related factors are:

1 The effects of migration

The UK has a history of both net immigration and net emigration, although the effect on **skill levels** is probably more important than the total numbers involved. The continuing removal of barriers to the free movement of labour in the EU is a major influence on migration levels. Internally, the **geographical distribution** of the workforce also affects firms' workforce planning. Recent trends include organisations moving to south-east England from other regions, and a general move by firms from city centres to save costs (further encouraged by developments in the infrastructure and in technology, enabling employees to work off-site).

	Inter-regional migration, 1997			**International migration, 1997**	
	Inflow (000)	**Outflow (000)**		**Inflow (000)**	**Outflow (000)**
North-East	39	45	England	257	192
North-West	107	117	Wales	11	4
London	167	222	Scotland	15	25
South-East	230	206	N. Ireland	2	3

Figure 6.1 *Migration, 1997*   Source: ONS

2 An ageing population

The average age of the UK's population is increasing. Effects on firms include changing demand levels for age-related goods and services, and pressure from the state for additional tax and other contributions to support the ageing population.

Share of population
Aged 65 and over, %

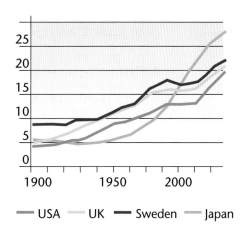

Figure 6.2 *Share of population aged 65 and over (%)*
Source: National Institute of Population and Social Security research

New working patterns

In Spring 1998, 44.6% of all female employees were working part time, compared with only 8.6% of all male employees (source, ONS).

Over 38% of part-time workers did not want a full-time post, compared with 23% who could not find one, Spring 1998 (source, ONS).

Workforce plans have to be amended to account for changes in working patterns. The traditional view of employment as a full-time permanent contract with a single employer is becoming outdated, as increasing numbers are being employed under new, more flexible, working arrangements.

- **Part-time work** has grown in importance throughout the economy: employers gain from increased flexibility, but now often have to provide the same conditions of employment for part-timers, which increases their costs.

- **Flexitime** has increased: employee morale improves through being able to adapt work to fit personal needs, but employers have to ensure that a 'core' of staff will be available during key periods.

- **Job sharing** – where two or more people share a full-time position – has grown in popularity: the employer faces additional administrative costs, offset by increased motivation of the job-sharing employees.

- **Fixed-term employment contracts** are often agreed: the employer has greater control over labour costs, and the employee may be motivated by the 'carrot' of a renewed contract.

> The labour market is becoming increasingly flexible, with two workers in five at present outside permanent employment. Benefits to a firm include lower total labour costs and a more flexible workforce.
>
> **KEY POINT**

Progress check

1 Why is workforce planning undertaken by a firm?

2 How will an organisation use STEP analysis to assess its labour force strategy?

2 To assess: social trends (e.g. part-time working); technological developments (e.g. new skills required); economic trends (e.g. levels of pay); political influences (e.g. changed employment regulations).

1 To counter loss of staff; to ensure production and other plans can be met; to respond to a changing environment.

6.2 Recruitment, selection and training

After studying this section you should be able to:

- *explain the value of efficient recruitment, selection and training to firms*
- *describe why firms undertake appraisal procedures*

LEARNING SUMMARY

Recruitment and selection

AQA	M2
EDEXCEL	M1
OCR	M2, M3
WJEC	M4
NICCEA	M2

Semi-skilled workers are likely to be recruited using local papers and Job Centres, whereas senior executives are more likely to be recruited nationally (or internationally) through 'headhunting' and national press advertising.

The interview has the advantage of being a two-way process but is not a reliable form of selection, often being subjective: there is no clear correlation between the ability to interview well and to do the job well.

Job descriptions and person specifications are prepared when recruiting staff.

The job description contains:
- post title and location
- summary of the task
- outline of work environment
- employment conditions.

The person specification contains:
- experience and qualifications required
- physical characteristics
- personality factors
- special aptitudes required.

External recruitment sources include advertising (local papers, national press or specialist publications), or using Job Centres, careers offices, employment agencies or executive search agencies ('head-hunters').

An alternative is to recruit **internally**, e.g. by promotion. The employee is known to the firm and will be familiar with work routines; staff morale and motivation improves; and it is less expensive. However, internal recruitment limits the firm's choice, and will not bring new ideas in from outside.

Interviews are the most popular selection method. They may be formal or informal, and conducted on a one-to-one or group basis.

The interviewer can assess:
- oral communication skills
- physical appearance
- personal attributes.

The interviewee can assess:
- physical working conditions
- future prospects
- the working atmosphere.

Other selection procedures include:
- **aptitude tests and simulations** used to test the candidate's skills and ability to carry out the duties of the post
- **achievement testing** to see if the candidate still has the relevant skills
- **personality tests** to measure the candidate's personality 'type'
- **intelligence tests** to check the candidate's reasoning and mental abilities.

The choice of selection procedure depends on its **suitability** for the post under consideration, its **cost**, its **coverage**, and the **time** available.

KEY POINT

Training and development

A typical induction programme includes information on the firm's history and present situation, a tour of the firm, meetings with relevant groups, and an identification of initial training and other needs.

Induction training introduces a new employee to the firm, and the firm to the new employee. Effective induction will make the employee comfortable – and therefore **motivated and productive** – as quickly as possible.

Internal (on-the-job) training is where employees learn as they work. Training is usually limited to particular skills or procedures, and uses work manuals. Internal training is easy to organise, it can be adapted to the trainee's needs, and is relatively inexpensive and job-specific. It can, however, disrupt work; the trainer may not possess adequate training skills and/or may be a poor communicator; bad work practices will be continued; and new approaches and methods are not introduced into the firm.

External, or **off-the-job**, training occurs where employees attend off-site training institutions (e.g. a local college). Advantages to the firm are that:

- specialist trainers are used
- training can be intensive
- general theories and ideas are introduced
- training occurs away from job distractions.

However, this training can be relatively expensive; it is isolated from work practicalities; and the trainee is away from the workplace and is not productive.

> **KEY POINT**
>
> The costs of **not** training include demotivated staff, poor production and productivity levels, increased accidents and absenteeism, dissatisfied customers, and loss of market share.

The **management by objectives** approach helps appraise performance, with employee achievement being measured against stated objectives. Performance appraisal is normally supported by an appraisal interview.

Appraisal

By appraising staff, managers seek to improve **present performance** levels through identifying individual strengths and weaknesses, and **future performance** by identifying individual potential for development.

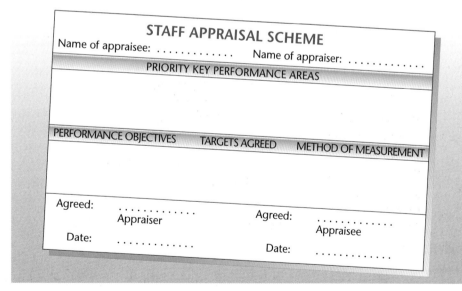

Figure 6.3 *Document from a company staff appraisal scheme*

Progress check

1 How does the Personnel department help a firm achieve labour targets?

6.3 Legislation at work

After studying this section you should be able to:

- *outline the main laws concerning employee and employment protection*
- *evaluate their effect on business*

LEARNING SUMMARY

Employee protection

AQA	M3
EDEXCEL	A2
OCR	M2, M3
WJEC	M4
NICCEA	M2

The Health and Safety at Work Act (HASAWA) 1974

Under HASAWA, employers must take **all reasonable care** to ensure the safety of their employees. They must provide appropriate training and instruction on health and safety matters, and are obliged to provide safe:

- working environments
- entry and exit arrangements
- plant and systems of work
- working processes (e.g. for unsafe materials).

The obligations of **employees** under HASAWA are:

- to co-operate with their employer on health and safety matters
- to take reasonable care of themselves and others at work
- not to interfere with anything provided for their safety
- to report defects in workplace equipment and processes.

Enforcement of HASAWA is carried out by the **Health and Safety Executive** (HSE), which carries out investigations by its inspectors, develops new health and safety laws and standards, and publishes guidance and advice.

The **Control of Substances Hazardous to Health** (COSHH) regulations are based on HASAWA provisions and require employers to control, monitor and carry out training associated with substances hazardous to employees' health.

Depending on its seriousness, a breach of HASAWA results in:

- a verbal warning
- issue of an improvement notice on the employer
- prosecution.

European Union health and safety protection

EU member states have **harmonised** health and safety provisions within a legal framework, adopting measures to ensure employers adopt safe practices.

The **Safety Framework Directive** outlines the responsibilities of employers and employees for encouraging workplace health and safety improvements. Specific protection includes covering:

- workplace requirements – e.g. fire safety and structural stability
- visual display units – covering design features of VDU work stations
- manual handling of heavy loads – employers must, where possible, provide mechanical assistance for handling heavy loads
- machinery safety – safety must meet harmonised EU standards.

The **Working Time Regulations** (1998) set minimum standards for employees (with some exceptions) for a maximum weekly working time: an average, including overtime, which does not exceed 48 hours.

The Working Time Regulations also establish minimum:

- rest periods – 11 consecutive hours per 24-hour period, a rest break where the working day exceeds 6 hours, and a 24-hour rest period in a seven-day period
- annual leave – a period of at least four weeks paid leave each year.

(United Kingdom)	Hours per week		
	Males	*Females*	*All*
Agriculture and fishing	49.1	43.9	48.2
Transport and communication	48.0	41.3	46.6
Energy and water supply	47.6	40.8	46.5
Construction	46.5	39.5	45.9
Distribution, hotels and restaurants	46.3	40.9	44.3
Manufacturing	45.3	40.7	44.2
Banking, finance and insurance	45.4	40.1	43.3
Public administration, education and health	44.4	40.9	42.4
Other services	45.3	41.0	43.5
All industries	**45.8**	**40.7**	**44.0**

The 44-hour average week represents a steady increase in hours worked from 42.6 (1984) and 43.7 (1990).

Over this period, full-time female employees have usually worked consistently, on average, around 5 hours a week fewer than men.

Figure 6.4 *Average weekly hours per full-time employee, Spring 1998*   Source: ONS, 1999

> Health and safety imposes **additional costs** (e.g. production costs rise). Firms also **gain**: a safe environment improves morale, and enhances the firm's reputation by avoiding bad publicity.   **KEY POINT**

Employment protection

AQA	M3
EDEXCEL	A2
OCR	M2, M3
WJEC	M4
NICCEA	M2

Remedies for unfair dismissal include **reinstatement**, if the employee wishes, **re-engagement** in a comparable job, or **compensation**.

Workers employed under a contract of service are protected against unfair dismissal. The employee can be dismissed for incompetence, gross or serious misconduct (e.g. assault, dishonesty), or the post becoming redundant.

Employers must give written particulars of the contracts of employment to employees within three months of starting work. Details included are:

- names of parties
- date employment commenced
- job title
- hours worked
- pay (rate, calculation, intervals)
- pension rights
- length of notice
- holidays and holiday pay
- sickness.

Recent EU measures being implemented in the UK include the:

- **Parental Leave Directive** – giving workers a right to at least three months' unpaid leave following the birth or adoption of a child
- **Part-time Work Directive** – providing for the equal treatment of part-time workers with full-time employees.

Discrimination

The **Sex Discrimination Acts** (1975 and 1986) make it unlawful for employers to discriminate on the grounds of sex when they advertise a job, recruit staff and set retirement dates. Exceptions exist, such as employing domestic servants.

The **Race Relations Acts** (1968 and 1976) make it unlawful for an employer to discriminate on the grounds of race, colour, nationality and ethnic origin. The 1976 Act established the **Commission for Racial Equality** which can investigate employers (and trade unions) believed to be acting in a discriminatory manner.

Figure 6.5 shows that, in every age group, unemployment rates are lower for white people than for people from each of the ethnic minority groups shown.

(Great Britain)	Percentages				
	16–24	*25–34*	*35–44*	*45 and over*	*All ages*
White	13	6	5	5	6
Black	39	18	12	16	19
Indian	18	7	6	7	8
Pakistani/Bangladeshi	29	16	13	26	21
Other groups	22	13	10	8	13
All ethnic groups	**14**	**7**	**5**	**5**	**7**

Figure 6.5 *Unemployment by ethnic group and age, 1997–98.*   Source: ONS, 1999

Equity, the actors' union, found (1999) that women receive 34% on average less than men for playing lead roles. Also in 1999, according to press reports, the three female members of Steps earned half the salaries their two male colleagues make.

The **Disability Discrimination Act** (1995) makes it unlawful for disabled persons to be treated less favourably than others. Employers must also review the work environment to help overcome problems faced by those with disabilities.

The **Equal Pay Act** (1970) requires employers to pay equal rates of pay to men and women doing the same job, or work of 'equivalent value'. This principle was reinforced by the EU in its 1975 Directive on equal pay.

According to the Equal Opportunities Commission (1999), the UK ranks tenth out of the 15 EU countries regarding equality of pay. Figure 6.6 shows that the pay gap between the sexes is narrowing: it fell from 20% to 19% from April 1998 to April 1999, according to the ONS. The minimum wage may continue this trend, since most low-paid workers are women.

In 1970, when the Equal Pay Act was introduced, women's average hourly pay was only 63% of men's. One factor in pay inequality may be that men and women tend to be employed in different occupations – for example, women dominate employment in the 'caring' professions – and 'mens jobs' tend to be higher paid.

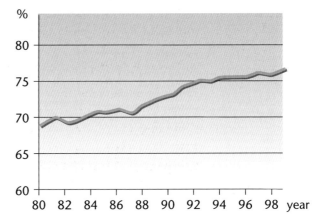

Figure 6.6 *Women's pay as percentage of men's pay.*   Source: ONS, 1999

> Issues of discrimination in business relate to an organisation's **social responsibility** and **ethical stance**. Evidence showing that discrimination still persists indicates that some firms must be criticised for their lack of social responsibility and inappropriate ethical behaviour.
>
> **KEY POINT**

Progress check

1 How do organisations benefit from operating safe practices?

2 What forms of discrimination still exist at work, and what legislation exists to counter them?

2 Racial – Race Relations Acts; sexual – Sex Discrimination Acts; Equal Pay Act; disability – Disability Discrimination Act.

1 Good publicity/avoiding bad publicity; improved employee morale; less time lost through accidents.

6.4 Motivation

After studying this section you should be able to:

- apply key motivation theories to the work of an organisation
- suggest how a firm can improve staff motivation in practice

Motivation theory

AQA	M2
EDEXCEL	M1
OCR	M2, M3
WJEC	M4
NICCEA	A2

When an employee is given a task to carry out, and it is carried out badly, this may be due to a lack of motivation rather than a lack of ability.

The work of the classical theorists is regarded as being limited, and has been modified by later theorists.

Theorists differ on what makes a job 'satisfying', such as:

- pay levels
- working hours
- work environment
- fringe benefits
- nature of work tasks
- management styles
- degree of job security
- promotion prospects
- organisational culture

Classical theory

These theorists studied organisational behaviour by examining the **nature of the work done**. **F W Taylor** used scientific management principles to separate jobs into their elements: this aspect of his work led to the development of work study and method study principles. Taylor believed that **high pay** acted as the prime motivator, largely ignoring morale and other influences.

Human relations and content theories

These theorists concentrate on people's **needs**, and not exclusively on the job being done, defining the organisation in terms of its **social environment**, and measuring both individual needs and how groups work together.

Elton Mayo researched into groups at the Hawthorne works of the Western Electric Company (1927 to 1932). He kept changing working conditions, discovering that output increased even when conditions worsened. His conclusions were that the employees being observed:

- were a tightly-knit group that enjoyed the attention being paid to them;
- which increased their self-esteem and, as a result, increased their output.

Abraham Maslow formulated 'his '**hierarchy of needs**' in the 1940s:

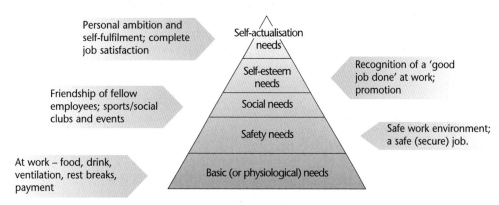

Figure 6.7 Maslow's hierarchy of needs

At any time, one group of needs is dominant, and the needs in this group must be met before the individual can proceed to the next group. In a work context, employees must be provided with the opportunity to fulfil these needs.

Maslow's ideas illustrate the importance of work to individuals, and help in explaining some of the social costs of high unemployment levels.

Frederick Herzberg analysed needs as **motivators**, which broadly relate to work content and to Maslow's higher-order needs, and **hygiene factors**, which relate to the working environment and to Maslow's lower-order needs. He suggests that, while hygiene factors should be present (motivation falls if they are neglected), they do not by themselves motivate employees.

Motivators	**Hygiene factors**
• achievement	• company policies
• recognition	• status
• responsibility	• supervision
• promotion	• security
• the work itself	• working conditions
	• money

> **KEY POINT**
> Herzberg's theory suggests that managers must provide motivators in the form of satisfying jobs, e.g. by using **job enrichment**, but must also ensure that negative hygiene factors do not detract from work being done.

Theory X links with the work of earlier classical theorists such as Taylor, emphasising money as the main motivating factor; Theory Y recognises (like Herzberg) the importance of Maslow's higher-order needs in motivating employees.

Douglas McGregor analysed two opposing attitudes concerning the formal organisation of workers. **Theory X** management – his negative attitude – assumes people dislike and will avoid work, and must be controlled and directed to get sufficient effort towards achieving organisational objectives. **Theory Y** management – the positive attitude – assumes employees can exercise their own control and direction, and can learn to seek and accept responsibility.

Supporters of Theory X argue an **authoritarian** form of organisational structure; supporters of Theory Y argue that the main limiting factors in a firm are management's ability and willingness to channel employee potential. Specific problems arise when employees expecting Theory Y management are subject to Theory X, or vice versa.

The Japanese approaches to management have been called '**Theory Z**', which recognises the Japanese emphasis on human relations at work and on employment for life.

Process theories

These theories analyse the thinking, or expectations, behind decisions made by employees. **V H Vroom's Expectancy Theory** argues that motivation depends on two factors: how attractive the outcome is, and the degree of expectation that the action will produce this hoped-for outcome. This theory suggests managers must analyse employees' motives, and ensure they have realistic goals to achieve.

Motivation in practice

AQA	M2
EDEXCEL	M1
OCR	M2, M3
WJEC	M4
NICCEA	A2

Management and leadership styles

A **democratic** manager (associated with Theory Y) guides and advises, but involves the group in decision-making. With **autocratic** management (linked to Theory X), the manager might allow group involvement, but decision-making stays at the top of the organisation. A *laissez-faire* manager chooses not to interfere in the work of the group: this approach can be successful if there are cohesive groups prepared to work in achieving common objectives.

The 'best' management/leadership style is determined by, for example:

- management training
- individual managers' preferences
- organisational size and complexity
- awareness of different styles
- organisational culture (see pages 45–6)
- stage of the organisation's evolution.

Overcoming poor motivation

Poor motivation causes employee dissatisfaction and alienation, leading to high labour turnover, increased absenteeism and sickness, poor timekeeping, and more disputes in the firm. Because these problems are not easily overcome, firms try to avoid them occurring in the first place through strategies such as:

- changing leadership styles – e.g. by moving towards a more democratic style
- establishing teamwork – to develop a sense of common purpose
- reviewing pay levels – also, perhaps, offering incentives or fringe benefits
- ensuring greater employee involvement – e.g. through quality circles
- job enrichment – giving employees the chance to use their full abilities.

This extract from BT's 1999 annual review illustrates a clear awareness of the importance of employee motivation:

> To help our people balance work and home responsibilities, we have a range of flexible working arrangements, including … part-time working and job sharing …
>
> BT encourages people to acquire shares in their company to enable them to share in its success …
>
> BT is an equal opportunities employer and is committed to developing a working culture which enables all employees to make their own distinctive contribution …
>
> BT runs a number of employee attitude surveys … Once feedback is received, managers work with their teams to explore any issues which may need attention …
>
> BT prides itself on being a 'learning organisation'. We spend around £180 million a year on the training and development of our people.

This EU Directive illustrates the drive nowadays to promote partnership between employers and employees.

To increase involvement and motivation, firms with over 1,000 employees in EU states (and at least 150 in each of two member states) must set up a works council or other procedure to inform and consult staff on key issues.

Remuneration

Examples of fringe benefits include a company car, subsidised meals and travel, and private health schemes.

Payment systems may be incentive-based (e.g. a piece rate per item produced) or time-based, such as an annual salary, or may combine the two (e.g. overtime at an increased hourly rate). Fringe benefits are also found.

The use of profit-sharing and share ownership schemes motivate employees by making them (feel) part of the firm's success. Such schemes now exist in about three-quarters of all UK public companies.

The £3.00 / £3.60 rate is below the £5.00 per hour figure campaigned for by many trades unions.

The UK now has a national minimum wage: the social purpose is to make all employers pay wages giving employees a basic standard of living. The UK, with its £3.60 an hour rate (£3.00 for 18- to 21-year olds) from April 1999, is now in line with the rest of the EU in having a minimum wage.

The Low Pay Commission is the body set up to oversee implementation of the minimum wage.

For the employer, wage costs may rise, affecting competitiveness: one way to cope with this increase would be to employ fewer staff. But by late April 1999, more than 1 million workers were still being paid below the legal minimum introduced at the start of the month.

Progress check

1 How should analysis of Herzberg influence the work of firms?
2 In what practical ways can a firm improve motivation?

2 Review: pay levels, level of involvement, management styles being used, feeling of job security, degree of recognition by others.

1 Ensuring positive hygiene factors (e.g. work conditions) and motivators (e.g. recognition) are both present for employees.

Sample question and model answer

1

Southern Foods plc is a large company with interests in food processing and the retail trade. Its directors are devising a new mission statement based on a draft submitted by the company's managing director. In its current mission statement the company seeks 'honourably to serve the needs of the community by providing products and services of superior quality at a fair price to all our customers'. The draft of the new mission statement includes references to environment concerns and to stakeholders other than customers.

(a) Explain what is meant by a mission statement. [2]

(b) Suggest reasons why the directors might be considering a reference to environmental concerns in its revised mission statement. [5]

(c) Suggest and justify amendments to the mission statement which might refer to a stakeholder other than a customer. [9]

(d) Suggest problems of motivation which might arise for assembly line workers employed in the food processing division of this firm. Evaluate methods of maintaining and improving motivation. [10]

Edexcel Specimen, Unit 1 Q1

> Only 2 marks are available, so the examiner expects a succinct definition.

(a) A mission statement summarises an organisation's key values and priorities.

(b) The present mission statement seems narrow in context and scope. Since Southern Foods has interests in food processing, it should acknowledge the concerns of customers and specific pressure groups (e.g. Friends of the Earth) regarding safe and environmentally-friendly food production. The company's staff may well share these concerns, and so the new mission statement could improve morale and motivation. There are defensive reasons: for example, to respond to competitors, and/or to avoid bad publicity, and a resultant fall-off in sales and profits, arising from environmental exploitation.

> The question does not state how many 'reasons': two may be sufficient if you clearly relate them to environmental issues and to the firm's situation.

(c) The question indicates that Southern Foods has interests in 'the retail trade'. It is therefore appropriate to extend the mission statement to include this fact, e.g. by recognising the importance of good relationships with local residents, and of working in partnership with local communities. The suggested amendment is that the company seeks 'to work with its local communities in supporting local needs, through conducting business ethically, and in giving proper regard for health, safety and the environment which is consistent with the commitment to contribute to sustainable development'.

> The examiner will expect you not only to identify a relevant stakeholder, but also to explain why your amendment is appropriate.

(d) Assembly line workers are likely to carry out repetitive, boring tasks: this is a common criticism of the flow-line method of production where the level of capital investment can determine what is done and how frequently it is done. The workers may be put on a new incentive scheme, such as 'piece-rate', but many motivation theorists argue that money is not necessarily the prime motivator. The company might consider implementing schemes such as job rotation – where the employees move between different jobs over a period of time – or job enlargement, where additional tasks and responsibilities are given, although this can be difficult to apply in certain mass-production situations. Improved working conditions – Herzberg's 'hygiene factors' – such as better ventilation, or additional 'perks' such as subsidised meals, may also help improve motivation. Another alternative is a more flexible approach to work, e.g. by implementing some form of 'flexitime' attendance: again, this can be difficult to achieve given that the method of production is continuous and therefore requires certain and regular staff numbers.

> Avoid merely reciting theorists: you must apply 'theory' to the situation.

Practice examination question

1 Read the extracts and answer all parts of the question which follows

---

Decline of full-time work to continue, says report

As government policies to create more flexible working take effect, forecasts indicate a continuing move in the labour market away from full-time employment. This shift has greatly increased feelings of job insecurity amongst employees.

Business leaders see growth in self-employment as a clear response to trends   5 such as job shedding. Dr Neil Blake, the report's research director, says: 'With employers creating almost no extra full-time jobs, 790,000 people will opt for self-employment between now and 2006. This enterprise activity is a positive response to the rationalisation, delayering and sub-contracting seen in many large UK firms.'   10

The report says that the fastest rise in employment will be for professional workers such as managers, solicitors and accountants.

Source: adapted from PHILIP BASSETT, Industrial Editor, The Times, 29 October 1996

Work 2000: new employers

An aspect of business reality is that women are half the workforce. A smart business supports women so that they can give their maximum to the organisation. A 'shift swap' scheme at Asda, the supermarket chain, enables, for example, a female cashier to work her weekly hours and attend her son's school concert. The Midland Bank raised its retention rate for women on maternity leave from 30% to 80% by allowing them to work flexibly on their return.

Source: adapted from JAYNE BUXTON, The Guardian, 6 January 1999

(a) What is meant by:

   (i)   'flexible working' (line 1);   [2]

   (ii) 'rationalisation' (line 9)?   [2]

(b) Examine the possible disadvantages for businesses of 'increased feelings of job insecurity amongst employees' (line 3).   [7]

(c) Many companies find that their existing employees do not have the appropriate skills for the future. Analyse how a company may overcome this problem.   [9]

(d) To what extent would the work of motivation theorists explain the new approach to women at work adopted by Asda and The Midland Bank?   [10]

AQA Specimen Unit 2 Q1

Chapter 7

Marketing

The following topics are covered in this chapter:

- Markets and market-led firms
- Market research
- The 'marketing mix'

7.1 Markets and market-led firms

After studying this section you should be able to:

- outline key features of the marketing function and market-led firms
- explain how firms segment their markets

Marketing function and objectives

AQA	M1
EDEXCEL	M2
OCR	M2, M3
WJEC	M2
CCEA	M3

The marketing function undertakes three key roles within an organisation:

- it supports the exchange process through **techniques aimed at the consumer**
- it **collects and analyses data** on both the consumer and the market
- it acts as a **co-ordinating function** for the organisation.

Marketing is the one function in an organisation that looks **outwards**: it integrates and co-ordinates by collecting, then disseminating, information on the consumer and the market throughout the organisation.

The traditional production-led manufacturing approach focused on the product. A **market-led** firm examines its activities through the eyes of its customers. It will set clear marketing **objectives**, and review its other objectives in the light of these: for example, a marketing objective to increase market share will affect other objectives, such as those based on production and cash flow.

The customer

Promote the product — Advertising, Sales promotion, Personal selling

Research the market — Collect market data, Record market data, Analyse market data

Place the product — Channels of distribution

Plan and develop — Identify customer requirements

Price the product — Penetration, Skimming

Produce the product — Incorporate customer requirements

Figure 7.1 *Marketing influence on the business cycle*

> The basis of the 'marketing concept' is that the customer is seen as the **start** of the business cycle, rather than its end.

Markets

Consumer markets exist for consumer goods, bought for their own satisfaction.

- **Single-use** consumer goods have short lives and are income-inelastic: often called **FMCGs** ('fast-moving consumer goods'), they satisfy physical (e.g. food), psychological (e.g. cosmetics), or impulse (e.g. sweets) needs.
- **Consumer durables** (e.g. DVD players, televisions) have an income-elastic demand: they are long-lasting, expensive, bought infrequently and with care.
- **Consumer services** – e.g. hairdressers, plumbers – are used more often as income grows, and tend to satisfy basic physical and safety needs.

Industrial markets contain products used by industries in their production.

> Industrial goods are classified as **capital goods** (e.g. new equipment), **industrial consumables** (e.g. fuel, stationery) and **industrial services** (such as cleaning).

	Consumer markets	*Industrial markets*
Customers	Many: allowing price to be set by the firm	Few: firm negotiates price and terms with the customer
Channel	Various, e.g. through wholesalers and retailers	Usually direct to customer
Product	More standardised: some differentiation	More personalised: may be made to end-user requirements
Methods	Resources concentrated on advertising: mass media used	Less generalised: more personal selling, use of specialist journals

Market segmentation

AQA	M1
EDEXCEL	M2
OCR	M2, M3
WJEC	M2
NICCEA	M3

Segmenting a market involves dividing it into distinct **subgroups**, using either the product or the consumer as the basis for segmentation.

Further education students	**Higher education students**	**Studying for the professions**	**Graduates**
Our Student Account – further education is the account for you if you are aged 16–19 and studying full-time for A-levels, BTEC, Advanced GNVQ, NVQ, City & Guilds or other similar qualifications	Our Student Package is for you if you are studying full-time for a degree or equivalent at a university or college of higher education in the UK	If you are studying full time for a professional qualification which will enable you to pursue your chosen career, this loan is available as an addition to our Student Package	If you've graduated within the last two years then our Graduate Package will give you the financial support you need during your first few years out from university or college

Figure 7.2 Barclays plc: product segmentation by consumer group (students), 1999

Consumers are often segmented according to the following **characteristics**:

1 Age

People's saving and spending habits change as they grow older.

> Banks, holiday firms and clothing manufacturers are examples of businesses targeting different age-related segments.

2 Sex

Some products (e.g. cosmetics) are gender-influenced; others may be targeted at one sex (e.g. brewers targeting certain brands of drinks at men, and other brands at women).

3 Socio-economic status

Marketers often use a scale to summarise occupational and social class groupings, identifying consumer groups by income and other characteristics (e.g. education, leisure interests).

How we see ourselves
% who describe themselves as

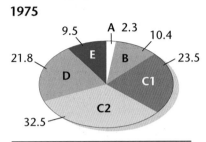

Source: British Election Study

Social grade
% of total population

1975

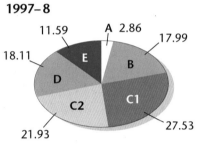

1997–8

Figure 7.3 Social grade

Source: NRS 1999

A Upper middle class
Higher managerial, administrative or professional

B Middle class
Intermediate managerial, administrative or professional

C1 Lower middle class
Supervisory or clerical and junior managerial, administrative or professional

C2 Skilled working class
Skilled manual workers

D Working class
Semi- and unskilled manual workers

E Lowest subsistence level
State pensioners or widows (no other earner), casual or lowest grade workers

4 National, regional and local factors

Income, tastes and leisure vary between cultures, and from area to area.

5 Psychographic profiling

These profiles use lifestyles to segment consumers and products: for example, differentiating a car by emphasising different features (safety, economy, styling, power, carrying capacity) to different 'lifestyle' customers (e.g. young single driver; family of four).

Firms concentrating on small market segments are carrying out **niche marketing**. They create a known name and image, and establish a market position. A small firm can compete in a market dominated by larger firms, and may find consumers will pay premium prices for its 'exclusive' product.

Problems for niche marketers are:

- the firm may have to remain small because overheads need to be kept low (if competitors benefit from economies of scale, they will be price-competitive);

- there is no diversification – the single-product approach depends for its success on consumer demand levels and tastes remaining at least constant.

> **KEY POINT**
> The targeted market segments influence the nature of the product, price, place and promotion used.

Progress check

1 How do consumer markets differ from industrial ones?

2 In what ways do marketers segment their markets?

2 Product characteristics; consumers (age, sex, income, lifestyle).

1 Number of customers; channels of distribution used; nature of product; methods used to advertise and sell.

7.2 Market research

- *explain how firms can analyse their market performance*
- *compare the relative benefits of field and desk market research methods*

Sources of information

AQA	M1
EDEXCEL	M2
OCR	M2, M3
WJEC	M2
NICCEA	M3

Firms need information about consumer habits and spending patterns, products, markets and the firm itself.

Firms use different methods to analyse their market performance.

SWOT analysis

This analyses a firm's **strengths** and **weaknesses**, which are mainly internal to the firm, and its **opportunities** and the **threats** to it, which are mainly external.

For example, a company selling garden sheds, which plans to diversify into greenhouses, could find that a SWOT analysis identifies these factors:

(S) – existing contacts/outlets; a known trade name; reputation for a quality product; existing suppliers of glass and wood; well-motivated employees.

(W) – employees lack suitable skills; no experience making glass-based products; no knowledge of the market for greenhouses; limited capital for expansion.

(O) – diversify to spread risk; expand capital through new share issue; reduce the seasonal effect of shed sales; no major local or regional competitor.

(T) – most competitors are large, so difficult to compete (fewer economies of scale) on price; uncertainty of climate change affecting long-term demand.

The Boston Growth and market share matrix

This matrix groups and analyses products under four headings:

The Boston Box analysis is particularly suitable for larger companies which have a wide product range.

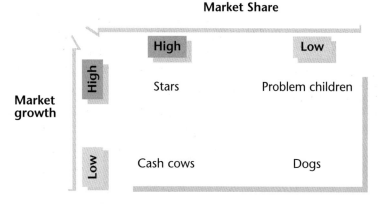

Figure 7.4 Boston Box analysis

- **'Stars'** are potentially highly profitable: large investment is needed to develop and promote them, and this should develop them into 'cash cows'.
- **'Problem children'**: in a slow-growth segment, they compete by plugging a hole in the product range but if not disposed of they can turn into 'dogs'.
- **'Cash cows'**: the key to the firm's profits and sales, it keeps investing in them, and they help finance the development of 'stars' – but if not managed properly they risk becoming 'dogs'.
- **'Dogs'** are heavy users of resources, but remain unprofitable: the firm rids itself of these unless there is a chance to make them profitable or they are being held for strategic reasons (e.g. to maintain market share).

The Boston Box technique is not a one-off approach to product analysis, since a product's status changes over time. It therefore illustrates the importance of having a **balanced product portfolio**.

Researching the market

AQA	M1
EDEXCEL	M2
OCR	M2, M3
WJEC	M2
NICCEA	M3

The purpose of market research is to **obtain information on market conditions** for the firm's products. It concentrates on three areas:

The product

- Who buys it, and how often do they buy?
- What stage is it at in its life-cycle?
- How does it fit into the product portfolio?
- Can it be improved or its life be extended?
- Is its price competitive?
- How effective is its promotion and distribution?
- How should any new products be – tested? – packaged? – launched?

The market

- What is its total size?
- How is it segmented?
- Is it expanding or contracting?
- Are there seasonal factors?
- Is it easy for new firms to enter?

The competition

- Who are the main competitors?
- What are their pricing policies?
- What promotion do they use?

The type of research

Field (or **primary**) research collects original data, using various techniques:

- **Questionnaires** are designed specifically for the task, and completed face-to-face, by telephone or through the post/e-mail.
- **Test marketing**: a potential new product is marketed regionally to gauge reaction to it, before committing the firm to production and national launch.
- **Consumer panels**: consumers who receive the product and comment on it.
- **Observation**: people's reactions (e.g. to a new display or form of packaging) are observed whilst they shop, to provide information from the marketplace.

Key decisions for the firm are to select the right people (the **sampling method**), and to select sufficient people (the **sample size**). The cost of collecting the data, and the time taken to collect it, are two key factors in the decision.

If field research is to provide relevant information, it must use a **representative sample**: consumers forming the sample must represent the market as a whole. The sampling method used may be **random** – where everyone in the population has an equal chance of selection – or **stratified** (a subgroup of the population is selected, e.g. using age or sex), or a **quota** may be set with data collected until the target quota is met. The larger the sample size, the more accurate are the results, but the more expensive and time-consuming it is to collect the data.

Firms undertake **quantitative** research – factual information (e.g. units sold, % of market share) – or **qualitative** research, which concentrates on attitudes and opinions (consumer tastes, likes and dislikes).

Desk (or **secondary**) research uses existing information such as the firm's own sales figures, official (e.g. Office of National Statistics) publications, trade associations and chambers of commerce, market research agency reports, and newspaper reports.

> **KEY POINT**
>
> Field research is tailored specifically to the product: most desk research is undertaken for other purposes so the data are not always relevant, although it is cheaper than field research and is normally quicker to obtain.

Progress check

1 How is SWOT analysis used by a firm?

2 How might a firm sample its potential market?

2 Use a random approach; stratify the sample; limit it by setting a quota.

1 It analyses its (internal) strengths and weaknesses, and opportunities and threats in the external environment.

7.3 The marketing mix

After studying this section you should be able to:

- *describe the four elements in the marketing mix*
- *outline the different approaches firms make concerning the product, its price, its distribution and promotion*

LEARNING SUMMARY

The product

AQA	M1
EDEXCEL	M2
OCR	M2, M3
WJEC	M2
NICCEA	M3

The product mix

A product may possess **core**, **secondary** and **tertiary** attributes – for example, freedom of movement may be a car's core attribute, with secondary attributes such as economy and reliability, and tertiary attributes of a warranty and the delivery date.

A firm's product mix – the complete range of products in all markets and segments – consists of different product lines (the group of products aimed at one market segment), the **mix width** identifying the number of product lines in this product mix: the wider the mix width, the more diversified the firm is and the better chance it has of surviving if a particular market segment collapses.

> Firms therefore **rationalise** their products, keeping them compatible if they cannot be placed in different market segments.

Each product line also has a **mix depth**: the number of different products in a single product line. The deeper the mix depth, the more segments the firm has to operate in to avoid its products competing with each other.

The product life-cycle

Firms develop new products to maintain a balanced product mix. A 'new' product may be **innovative** (the original model/type, e.g. the Sony Walkman), an **imitative** product which copies the original one, or a **replacement** (new model).

A product has only a limited life once it is introduced on the market. It is therefore important that a firm has a balanced product portfolio (product mix), replacing those in the maturity and decline stages with newer products.

1 Introduction

Following planning and development, the product is introduced onto the market. Characteristics of this stage are:

- low initial sales, due to limited knowledge and no consumer loyalty
- heavy promotion to build brand image and consumer confidence
- losses (low profits at best) due to heavy development and promotion costs
- limited distribution levels, but high stockholding for the manufacturer.

Attempts are made to gain market share (e.g. through penetration pricing – see page 114), but there remains a high chance of product failure.

2 Growth

> The product is changing from a 'star' into a 'cash cow'.

As consumer knowledge and loyalty grow, the firm increases sales and starts making profits (helped by economies of scale). Competitors may introduce similar products, or adapt their price and promotion policies.

3 Maturity

Growth slows as the product reaches saturation sales level. Profits are being maximised, but the firm has to fight to defend its market position. Sales are maintained by promotion, customer loyalty (repeat purchases) and product differentiation (see page 112) through alterations such as new packaging.

4 Decline

Total sales fall for the firm (and often the industry). To counter this, the firm may reduce prices, cutting into its profit margin. Production may be maintained if other firms abandon their products, in an attempt to gain a larger share of the (smaller) market. The firm may also undertake niche marketing in a particular market segment.

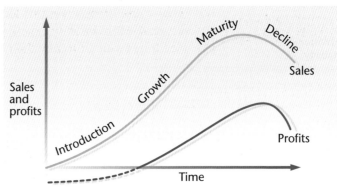

Figure 7.5 *Stages of the product life-cycle*

Extending product life

> By extending product life, the firm hopes to extend the maturity (high-profits) stage.

The firm may try extending an existing product's life by altering:

- the **product** – renewing the image (a 'new improved' model); introducing new models such as a diesel engine version of a car; extending the product into other formats (e.g. ice-cream Mars, originally just a chocolate bar)
- the **marketing strategy** – changing the image or appeal (e.g. personal computers being used for games/leisure as well as for work).

> An example of change is Volkswagen's purchase of Skoda in the 1990s, which has led to improved, renewed product and image.

Product life-cycle analysis has been criticised for overstating the importance of developing new products rather than seeking to extend the lives of existing ones: new product development is risky and expensive. Also, the four stages are not always easily separated, and the life-cycle can become a self-fulfilling prophecy.

> **KEY POINT**
>
> Product life-cycle analysis determines other aspects of marketing policy, e.g. how the product is advertised, distributed, priced and developed.

Product differentiation and branding

Product differentiation explores **how consumers view products**. A highly differentiated product is regarded as distinct, having no near substitutes. The product may be different (e.g. it is better designed or made), or may be **perceived** as different, due to psychological factors such as advertising or branding. Product differentiation is helped where a product has a **unique selling point** (USP), a feature which the firm can focus on to differentiate it from competitor products. Again, the USP may be based on an actual difference (e.g. quality), or on a perceived difference which is enhanced by persuasive advertising.

> Specific brand and trade names often used to describe all products of the same type include 'biro', 'hoover', 'tarmac', 'jiffybag' and 'jeep'.

Branding assures consumers that their next purchase of the branded item will be virtually identical to their last purchase. This consistency creates **brand loyalty**, giving the manufacturer the opportunity to highlight and advertise apparent differences between products. Through branding:

- a respected brand name helps the manufacturer sell new products
- there is the promise of repeat purchases through brand loyalty
- retailers will give display space to the branded product
- the brand name can be placed in another market
- market segmentation becomes easier.

> An example is when Unilever plc bought Colman's mustard, it re-marketed it and then launched other foodstuffs using the well-known Colman's name.

Own-label brands – goods branded with the retailer's name – have increased in popularity. The retailer can buy from a manufacturer after agreeing quality standards, rather than buying at high prices from a major brand supplier, and then sell the own-brand goods at competitive prices. The manufacturer can benefit from using excess production capacity.

Branding relies on packaging. Originally there just for protection, the packaging now carries the brand name or logo, gives product information that must be legally displayed, and offers space which can be used by the manufacturer to persuade the consumer to buy the product.

> Modern packaging offers a **communication base**, ease of **display**, **impact**, and **environmental acceptability**.

Pricing decisions

AQA	M1
EDEXCEL	M2
OCR	M2, M3
WJEC	M2
NICCEA	M3

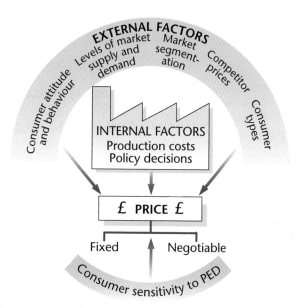

Figure 7.6 *Price influences*

Pricing methods

Chapter 1 (see page 24) explained how economists view price as the interaction of supply and demand. Many marketers regard this analysis as useful but limited, arguing that the role of other factors such as promotion are understated.

> Many small retailers simply add a fixed percentage mark-up to the cost they have paid for goods bought for re-sale.

Chapter 5 (see page 87) outlined how costs influence price. **Cost-based** pricing uses production and other costs: an example is **cost-plus** pricing, which is based on **absorption costing** and takes all costs into account:

- the product's direct costs are calculated
- its share of indirect costs (overheads) are added
- a percentage (the mark-up) is added for profit, to give the selling price.

Contribution pricing is an alternative cost-based approach: it uses **marginal costing** principles and links to break-even analysis, calculating the contribution (see page 88) to total fixed costs made from each product sold. As long as the selling price exceeds the product's variable costs, it is making a contribution towards fixed costs. The firm uses this information to make pricing decisions, such as setting **differential** prices or selling **loss leaders**.

> Rail and airline transport is a good example: low-fare, stand-by, off-peak or customer category (e.g. as 'students' or 'senior citizens') pricing is used to fill seats: the marginal cost of these passengers is low, and any contribution helps cover fixed costs.

> **KEY POINT**
>
> A firm using cost-based pricing will ensure that all its costs are met by its selling price, but – if it ignores competitors' prices in the market – it may lead to an uncompetitive price being set.

Market-based pricing occurs when firms set their prices at or near the current market price. The firm can set a competitive price: where there is little product differentiation in the market and therefore a high elasticity of demand, the firm has to charge virtually the same price as competitors. Where a competitor is the brand leader, the firm may have to sell at a lower price to achieve an acceptable sales level. The firm may try to establish a profit-maximising price, by taking into account the product's elasticity of demand.

Pricing strategy

A firm must also consider its pricing strategy. It may consider psychological pricing, setting a price to reflect the product's image and its target market expectations. Consumers expect to pay more for certain brand names (e.g. Dior, Chanel, Nike, Mercedes), the high price reinforcing the quality image.

A skimming or 'creaming' strategy is where a high price is set for a new, innovative product to maximise profits in the short-term. This is possible because the product has a scarcity value, the high price boosts its image and appeal, and the firm is in a temporary monopoly position. Once competitors arrive onto the market (often encouraged by the high price and profit margin), the firm will normally cut the price and focus on the mass market.

A penetration pricing strategy is one of lower prices and profit margins, and is used with both new and established products. The purpose is to increase market share. Penetration pricing is often used:

- with products that are high-volume, long-life and price-sensitive
- if the firm wishes to become market leader, has a cost advantage over its competitors, or can benefit from economies of scale.

Predatory pricing is a form of penetration pricing where a low price, often below the cost of production, is set in order to drive competitors out of the market. This anti-competitive strategy can be used if a conglomerate decides to cross-subsidise its predatory pricing in one market with profits from elsewhere. For example News Corporation, owners of *The Times* newspaper, cut its weekday price in September 1993 from 45p to 30p – and later to as low as 10p – following a trial in the Kent area (which had reportedly increased sales by 14 per cent). This was seen by some commentators as predatory pricing based on cross-subsidy from News Corporation's other activities, in an attempt to gain more of the 'quality' newspaper market segment by capturing the market share of competitors such as *The Independent*.

The benefits of penetration pricing can be quick growth for the firm, coupled with eliminating competitors from the market and discouraging new firms from entering. It is also a high-risk strategy: cutting prices also cuts profit margins and affects liquidity if the product's demand is more inelastic than expected. Competitors may respond by cutting prices, resulting in a price war.

Another psychological influence is to set a price below a key figure: e.g. £9.95 rather than £10.00.

Examples of skimming strategies are often found with technological developments: early calculators were extremely expensive prestige items.

Penetration pricing is a useful strategy if brand loyalty can be established, but psychologically a low price can be associated with low quality in consumers' minds.

> **KEY POINT**
> Price represents a profit objective to the seller and a measure of value to the buyer.

Place

Physical distribution involves delivering the correct quantity of goods whilst maintaining the product's quality and security. All distribution channels offer a level of **effectiveness** which must be offset against their **cost**. Choice of channel also depends on the degree of outlet **control** required: mass-market items such as newspapers are not affected by the outlet's image, whereas technically complex or 'exclusive label' products are distributed with the manufacturer exerting much greater control over the number and quality of the outlets.

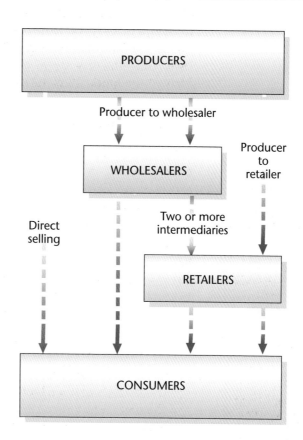

Figure 7.7 *Channels of distribution*

Many products are sold **directly** from producer to consumer. Examples include 'factory shops', and many industrial goods. Benefits to the seller include greater profit through avoiding intermediaries, and close customer contact.

The **producer-wholesaler** channel is popular with small producer firms making a limited product range. Wholesalers provide several valuable services:

- **bearing risk** of not selling the goods – the producer has a guaranteed market
- **storing** the goods – the producer's stockholding costs are reduced
- **advising** the producer on market performance
- **promoting** the product.

However, the producer loses control over the final product outlets and receives lower profit margins (compared with direct selling).

The traditional wholesaler channel is inappropriate for major high-street chains such as Asda and Tesco, who operate their own warehouses which break bulk for despatch to the outlets. Other forms of producer-retailer link include the **tied outlet** approach operated by brewers and petrol producers.

The full chain is still used, normally where products are sold through smaller retailers. The wholesaler allows wide product distribution without the producer having major transport and administrative costs: but the producer again lacks control over promotion, and contact with the final consumer.

E-commerce

Tesco has introduced internet shopping into over 100 stores following its success in 30 supermarkets, where it accounted for about 7% of turnover. A likely distribution development is the use of a centralised warehousing system.

An estimated 43% of the UK was wired up for internet use by 2000. Some internet-based firms such as Kitbag Sports and the share dealing service E-trade have become established, and high-street names such as Tesco, Dixons, Argos and Iceland have established web-sites, with competitors following suit for defensive reasons. Other technological developments include **Open**, digital TV's electronic shopping mall.

> Internet- and TV-based distribution allows firms closer access to the final market, and greater access (through 24-hour trading).
>
> **KEY POINT**

Promotion

AQA	M1
EDEXCEL	M2
OCR	M2, M3
WJEC	M2
NICCEA	M3

The **promotion mix** consists of 'above-the-line' costs (advertising), and 'below-the-line' costs – personal selling, sales promotions, and other influences such as packaging and public relations: the mix chosen depends on relative cost and effectiveness.

Firms promote their products to sell them in the existing (or a different) market or segment, to introduce new products onto the market, and to compete with others to maintain or increase market share. A firm may also advertise to improve its **corporate image**, which can positively boost its whole product range, or counter negative publicity or image problems.

Promotion can be analysed using techniques such as **AIDA**: it must

- create **awareness** of the product/brand in the market-place
- arouse the **interest** of the consumer
- stimulate **desire** for the product/brand in the consumer
- provoke **action** by the consumer.

A firm can also measure **advertising elasticity**: the extent to which changes in advertising spending affect demand. If a small change in advertising spending leads to a large change in demand, the firm has an advertising-elastic product.

The advertising message

Advertising is a media-delivered message paid for by a sponsor. **Informative** advertising provides factual information about the product. Most advertising campaigns contain some information, and also an element of **persuasion**. The objective of persuasive advertising is to convince customers that they need the product: it includes persuading them to buy the firm's product rather than a rival one. Persuasive advertising is assisted by the use of branding and other forms of product differentiation, seeking to establish brand image and customer loyalty through repeating its persuasive statements.

Persuasive advertising is often criticised for:

- **making outlandish claims** – false claims are illegal under the Misleading Advertising Directive (EU) and the Trade Descriptions Act (see pages 68 and 69), and are monitored by the **Advertising Standards Authority**'s code of practice
- **manipulating consumers** – tactics involving sex or status are used to make the product more appealing.

Ethically-aware firms will adopt advertising campaigns that avoid criticism under these headings.

The advertising medium

Television and radio

Commercial stations provide mass coverage and are therefore suitable for mass-appeal goods. Drawbacks include the expense (of TV advertising), the increasing tendency of viewers to channel-hop and avoid adverts as the number of available stations increases, the temporary nature of the advert, and the lack of selectivity of this approach.

Print-based media

This advertising is more permanent – the advert can include a reply slip and be kept for future reference. It also provides more detail than broadcast advertisements, and allows advertisers to target certain groups (e.g. special-interest magazines). It is less expensive than TV advertising, though it lacks the impact of sound and movement.

In 1999, German company DVAG paid over £5 million to put its name for three years on an approximately 10 centimetre-wide by 4 centimetre-deep space on Michael Schumacher's baseball cap.

Other media

These include cinema advertising, the internet, posters, and **direct marketing** such as leaflets and mailshots (i.e. direct mail, also known as 'junk mail', which indicates its very low response rate).

> **KEY POINT**
> The firm can choose from a variety of media, the main limiting factor being the size of the advertising budget. Other influences include the market (its nature and size) and the product.

An **advertising campaign** puts the firm's advertising strategy into operation. Larger firms can afford to employ specialist advertising agencies – a marketing economy of scale (see page 56) – to create their advertising campaigns.

Below-the-line promotion

Firms use **sales promotion** – short-term incentives – to encourage new purchasers to try their products, and/or to reinforce existing customers' brand loyalty. The main sales promotion techniques are:

Sales promotion can be used to gain additional market share, or for a more defensive reason (e.g. by responding to a competitors promotion).

* **free samples** to encourage the customer to try the product, and help establish brand loyalty
* **price reductions** and **premium offers**, e.g. the use of free gifts, discount or money-off coupons, to encourage customers to repeat the purchase
* **loyalty cards** to encourage consumers to build up company loyalty (and therefore boost own-brand and overall sales)
* **competitions** which act as an inducement to buy the product
* **after-sales service** to persuade customers to buy a particular brand.

POS is particularly popular with firms selling impulse-purchase products such as sweets.

Point-of-sale (POS) advertising is used in conjunction with sales promotion. POS includes any merchandising that takes place at the point of sale: it tends to concentrate on packaging and display to provide product recognition.

Advertising is impersonal, being directed at a mass audience. A benefit from **personal selling** is that the firm can **target its message** to suit the recipient. Through individually tailoring its message, the firm has close control over its promotion, e.g. by employing the sales staff or agents. It also receives directly any consumer comments, and its sales staff can handle non-sales matters such as customer queries. The main disadvantage of personal selling is its high cost. Other drawbacks include the relatively high staff turnover and lack of continuity.

> **KEY POINT**
> Effective promotion relies on effective communication to tell consumers about products: the communication often consists of both informative and persuasive elements.

Progress check

1 How can a firm use product differentiation in its marketing?
2 What pricing policies are available to firms?

2 Cost-based (cost-push, contribution); market-based (competitive; psychological; profit-maximising; skimming; penetration).
1 Product differentiation – how consumers view products – helps firms promote products by focusing on actual or perceived differences.

Sample question and model answer

1

Read the following passage and then answer the questions that follow.

> First sold over 60 years ago by Rowntree Mackintosh, Smarties are a strong brand in an established part of the confectionery market targeted at children. They are normally sold in tubes, multi-packs (three tubes), mini-cartons and cartons. The Mars bar is another popular confectionery brand, made and sold with companion products, which include Twix and Maltesers. A recent entrant to the market was when Mars launched M&Ms – a major seller in the USA, and very similar to Smarties – onto the UK market.

(a) Outline briefly the influences on Rowntree Mackintosh when deciding to sell Smarties in a variety of packaging sizes. [4]

(b) Rowntree Mackintosh and Mars are examples of 'market-led' companies. What are the main objectives of such companies? [4]

(c) How might the marketing mix adopted by Rowntree Mackintosh for Smarties alter as a result of Mars introducing M&Ms into the UK? [6]

The examiner expects a short answer only. Remember to consider legal aspects as well as marketing ones.

(a) Rowntree Mackintosh would have been influenced by the possibility of producing different packs for different market segments: aesthetics (the attractiveness of different package designs); the cost of raw materials; the varieties of competitor packaging; EU and other regulations concerning product labelling and safety; and general storage/protection requirements.

It is worth contrasting a market-led approach with a production-led one.

(b) The main objectives of a 'market-led' company focus on the consumer or 'client'. The objectives will probably refer to the size of the market, the clients' wants in this market, how the company can meet these wants, and targets that are set to achieve this. This approach contrasts with the more traditional 'production-led' approach, where the product is made and then put onto the market: unlike a market-led company, where the end user is of primary concern, a production-led company tends to be more concerned with the ease and efficiency of making the product.

There are two elements in this part: you should first make **general** comments (e.g. a general definition of marketing mix), and then focus on the **particular** illustration given, by working through each 'P' at a time.

(c) 'Marketing mix' refers to the 'four Ps': product, price, place and promotion. It identifies these elements, and the relative importance given to each by a firm's marketing function.

Rowntree Mackintosh would have considered the effect of M&Ms on its product, and whether Smarties needed re-styling (e.g. through new packaging, or aiming its product at the adult market). It would also examine the relative prices of the two products, and may find it has to adjust the price of Smarties to compete on a price basis with M&Ms. Third, it would examine its channels of distribution ('place'), comparing the nature and efficiency of these channels with those used by its rival. Finally, Rowntree Mackintosh would review its promotion strategies to see how best to respond to the new product and its associated advertising/promotion.

Practice examination question

1 Study the information below and then attempt all parts of the question.

Smythe plc is based in the UK and makes shirts. Production capacity is 400,000 units per annum. Sales volume is currently 145,000 per annum. The shirts are sold by Smythe to retailers at a price of £16 each.

Table 1 Smythe's cost structure

	Cost per unit
Variable costs:	
Labour	£3.00
Maintenance	£0.60
Materials	£2.80
Overhead cost per unit (at maximum capacity)	
Total overhead per unit	£2.91

Most economic forecasters expect the £ to decrease in value over the next three years as measured against the Euro and most major foreign currencies.

Smythe is considering increasing its production level to maximum capacity and attempting to sell in the lower-priced market segments, possibly under a different brand name, whilst retaining existing sales.

Table 2 UK Shirt market by sector

sales volume	price to retailer	market % supplied by importers	retailers
175 million	£4–£6	80%	supermarkets, chain stores, mail order
20 million	£8–£13	12%	multiple tailors independents
5 million	£14–£18	3%	prestigious department stores, and other quality outlets

(a) Explain the term 'variable costs' as used in Table 1. [4]

(b) Define and then calculate for Smythe's shirts:
   (i) the break-even level of output; [6]
   (ii) the current margin of safety. [4]

(c) Smythe is considering selling in the lower-priced market segments. Discuss whether this is likely to be successful. [15]

OCR Specimen, Business Decisions unit, Q1

Chapter 8

Productive efficiency

The following topics are covered in this chapter:

- Organising production
- Capacity utilisation
- Controlling stock
- Quality management

8.1 Organising production

After studying this section you should be able to:

- compare the characteristics of job, batch and flow production in the context of business
- assess the relevance of lean production to today's firms

LEARNING SUMMARY

Methods of organising production

AQA	M2
EDEXCEL	M2
OCR	M2, M3
WJEC	M5
NICCEA	M3

This can prove difficult: for example, in 1993 Eurotunnel had to find an extra £0.8 billion to fund the **cost** of the Channel Tunnel, and postponing the Tunnel's opening (**completion**) put an extra pressure on the company's **cashflow**.

Job production

Production of goods and services is either **intermittent** or **continuous** in nature.

Job production involves the output of a **single product** to **individual specifications**: examples include the construction of a single machine tool, a ship, the Millennium Dome and the Severn Bridge. Firms using job production have to estimate accurately the 'three Cs': **costs, cashflows** and **completion date**.

Characteristics of job production are:

a high-priced product

made with

equipment flexible enough to meet individual job demands

used by

highly skilled and versatile labour

supervised by

centralised management

who use

techniques to plan and monitor the production process.

Examples include producing batches of bread and cakes, and making a number of furniture items to the same design.

Batch production

A quantity of a product is made without using a continuous production process. The characteristics are similar to job production, although unit costs are normally lower since fixed costs are spread over the number of items in the batch. The production area is often organised by grouping together similar machines and processes such as welding and assembly.

An **economic batch quantity** (EBQ) can be calculated by using the same formula as EOQ (see page 126):

$$EBQ = \sqrt{\frac{2bd}{h}}$$

where: b = batch setting-up costs
d = demand
h = holding costs

Mass (or flow) production

Examples include cars, televisions, washing machines and other consumer durables.

This involves the output of **identical, standardised products** using continuous production with highly specialised inputs, each being employed continually on the same operation. Mass production relies on the support of an advanced marketing function and is associated with products having high and long-term levels of demand. It is also associated with problems of low morale arising from worker boredom, and with production stoppages through equipment failure.

Its characteristics are:

- a lower-priced product (compared with those made using job production)
- a greater proportion of semi-skilled or unskilled labour
- high capital investment costs, offset by economies of scale
- specialised plant and equipment having relatively little flexibility
- production layout that minimises the movement of parts and sub-assemblies
- highly automated production and assembly lines
- costs being subject to standard costing and budgetary control procedures.

Mass production is based on **specialisation** and the **division of labour**, which create surpluses that can then be traded internationally.

Compared with job production, this method is usually more cost-effective, but this extra **productivity** means a loss of **flexibility** (of both capital and labour). Firms using mass production may find it difficult to respond to changing market – and therefore production – requirements. The drawbacks of mass production therefore include low morale, lack of flexibility of labour and machinery, and major production stoppages through equipment failure. This has led to the Japanese-influenced development of **lean production** (see page 124) to eliminate wastage of materials and time and to develop a more flexible approach.

Products made using mass and lean production techniques are widely found in international trade. Governments will want to ensure that their industries are competitive internationally.

International productivity (cars per worker)

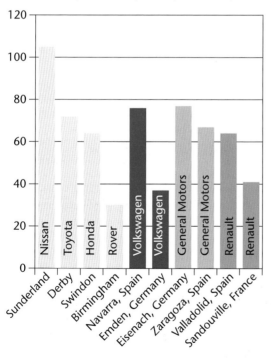

National productivity (UK = 100)

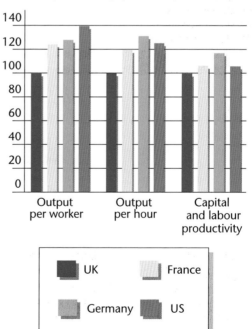

Figure 8.1 *National and international productivity, 1998*　　　*Source (international): NIESR*

> The types of production system normally depend on the **scale of production** being used, and will themselves influence the **physical layout** of the production area.
>
> **KEY POINT**

Lean production

AQA	M2
EDEXCEL	M2
OCR	M2, M3
WJEC	M5
NICCEA	M3

The 'lean production' approach seeks to improve the use of a firm's productive resources in order to:

- reduce wastage, stockholding and other costs
- improve labour productivity levels
- increase capacity utilisation (see page 124)
- improve quality (see page 128)
- heighten employee morale through involvement and input.

By achieving this, the firm will be in a better position to respond to changes in its market. Key elements in a lean production approach include the following.

Cell production

A development from mass production, this manufacturing approach divides a continuous production line into 'cells', self-contained units producing an identifiable section of the finished item. In this way, staff in the cell are made to feel more involved in the firm's production.

Continuous improvement

Kaizen is a Japanese term describing a philosophy that investing in employees' views and ideas can often be more productive than investing in new equipment. Widely introduced in UK firms in the 1990s, Kaizen groups are set up throughout the firm: e.g. a shop-floor production cell may operate as a Kaizen team. These groups meet regularly to discuss production and other problems, and to offer solutions.

The Kaizen philosophy stresses that an employee has two jobs: carrying out the job, and also looking for ways to improve it.

For Kaizen to be implemented successfully:

- employees must be willing and motivated to make contributions
- employees must work in teams (such as a production cell)
- the firm's organisational culture must support its implementation.

> The Kaizen philosophy is not limited to production: it is based on many small improvements being identified and implemented throughout the firm, by staff in all functions.
>
> **KEY POINT**

Just-in-time (JIT)

This approach is based on the wish to reduce stockholding costs by, if possible, operating with a zero buffer stock. To do this, a firm must establish close working relationships with the suppliers of its stock, since frequent deliveries of satisfactory-quality stocks are needed for JIT to function efficiently.

Advantages of JIT

- Holding and storage costs are cut
- Fewer problems of wastage and rotation
- Liquidity improves
- Quicker response to market change

Disadvantages of JIT

- Order processing costs increase
- Total reliance on the supplier
- Delivery problem stops production

One feature of JIT is the **kanban** order card system. An example is where components are stored in two bins: when one is emptied, it – with its kanban card – is taken to where the component is made. The component is manufactured, 'just-in-time' for when it is needed in production (as the other bin becomes empty).

The kanban system therefore involves employees to a greater extent in the production process.

Flexible specialisation

This approach argues that, since the tastes and demands of today's customers change regularly, production must be able to respond quickly and flexibly to these changes. Traditional flow-line production, with its emphasis on making a single product continuously, is not well equipped to meet this because its machines are too specialised and labour is insufficiently skilled.

Firms wishing to adopt this manufacturing approach face certain costs. Capital investment is needed in flexible (e.g. reprogrammable) machinery and equipment, and the need to develop a multi-skilled and versatile workforce means extra and improved training for existing employees (which may mean extra wage costs), as well as a review of the firm's recruitment policies of new staff.

> Flexible specialisation changes the emphasis from mass back to batch production.

Time-based management

Managers are encouraged to consider managing time in the same way that they manage the firm's human and physical resources. Encouraging managers to concentrate on time-based management should lead to shortened production times (e.g. machinery set-up times), which in turn:

> Productivity should also increase as a result of shorter production times.

- reduce stockholding costs – lower stocks are held because the firm can be more responsive to market changes by having shorter production runs
- improve customer satisfaction, because the firm can meet their orders more quickly.

> **KEY POINT**
>
> Successful lean production results in producing more, and making it more efficiently, by using less (fewer resources).

Progress check

1 State the likely traditional production methods for these:
(a) six identical houses being built on a new estate; (b) an extension to an existing house on the estate; (c) the cars owned by the householders.

2 How does a 'continuous improvement' approach operate?

3 Identify why 'Just-in-time' production is becoming increasingly popular.

3 Advantages of lower stockholding and other costs; less wastage; quicker response time to market changes.

2 Teams review problems and make suggestions for solution. Management adopts and reviews solution with teams.

1 (a) batch; (b) job; (c) mass.

8.2 Capacity utilisation

After studying this section you should be able to:

- *calculate a firm's capacity utilisation*
- *explain the relevance of high and low utilisation in business*

High and low utilisation

AQA	M2
EDEXCEL	M2
OCR	M2, M3
WJEC	M5
NICCEA	M3

Capacity utilisation measures actual output as a percentage of maximum output. A firm's productive capacity is based on its **resources**: in particular, its premises, capital equipment and labour. When all are working at maximum output, the firm is operating at **full capacity** (it has 100% capacity utilisation).

The formula for calculating capacity utilisation is:

$$\frac{\text{present output}}{\text{maximum output capacity}} \times 100$$

It appears that Courtmills (see page 91) has a capacity utilisation of 80%, based on its projected 80,000 output and maximum capacity of 100,000; and Smythe (see page 119) has a capacity utilisation of 36.25%, assuming that 145,000 sales equals output, compared with a maximum capacity of 400,000.

> As an example, if £100,000 fixed costs are spread over a maximum output of 20,000, the unit fixed cost is £5: spread over, say, 50% capacity utilisation (10,000 items), the fixed cost rises to £10 per unit.

Why is capacity utilisation important? A firm incurs fixed costs (see page 88), which do not change in the short-term as output changes. **If the firm can spread these fixed costs over greater output, unit costs will fall.**

The higher the capacity utilisation, therefore, the lower unit costs should be – not just because unit fixed costs fall, but also because of economies of scale, which **reduce unit variable costs** (e.g. through bulk-buying raw materials).

Working at or near full capacity can also create pressures for a firm:

- pressure on machinery – e.g. maintenance is difficult because the machines are always needed for production
- pressure on employees – e.g. absenteeism due to increased stress caused by high workloads.

By operating at or near full capacity, the firm also finds it hard to cope with any additional work. It can achieve additional capacity, e.g. by employing part-time staff (a strategy often used by particular industries, e.g. seasonal-based ones) and/or using extra capital resources (e.g. hire of machines or premises). This gives some **flexibility** in meeting changing demand and market conditions.

> Reducing capacity is often referred to as **rationalisation**: where major restructuring occurs and jobs are lost, the terms **downsizing** or **right-sizing** are sometimes used.

Figure 8.2 illustrates **low capacity utilisation**. This low utilisation brings problems such as either absorbing higher unit fixed costs through accepting lower profit margins, or passing them on as higher selling prices. A firm can increase utilisation by taking measures to **boost product demand** where it has fallen temporarily: e.g. advertising campaigns, special offers, price reductions, etc. It can also increase utilisation by **reducing excess capacity** if demand has fallen permanently: strategies include not replacing leavers ('natural wastage'), cutting shifts, and moving to cheaper premises or otherwise cutting fixed costs.

> As capacity utilisation increases, unit fixed costs fall; as capacity utilisation falls, unit fixed costs rise.

KEY POINT

Figure 8.2 Over-capacity in the European car industry

The role of technology in productive efficiency

The role of the production function is to turn input into output as efficiently as possible: this is a measure of the firm's **productivity**. Labour productivity is the most common measure: falling productivity makes a firm, industry or country uncompetitive, whereas rising productivity improves competitiveness.

It is also important for a firm's **capital** to be productive. Many firms benefit from using new technologies in the production process.

- **Computer-aided design** (CAD) packages generate efficient product designs that can be altered immediately, e.g. using light pens or touch-sensitive screens
- **Computer-aided manufacture** (CAM) uses and links robotics and other forms of automation
- **Computer-integrated manufacture** (CIM) takes this further by integrating all aspects of production, e.g. production control with stock ordering.

> One problem with rising labour productivity is that it may lead to job losses, since fewer employees are now required to produce the same output.

> This illustrates how capital is substituted for labour: whilst the firm's productivity and efficiency may improve, there is a corresponding **social cost** of increased unemployment.

Progress check

1 Outline why a firm seeks to maximise its capacity utilisation.

2 How can technological developments improve productive efficiency?

2 CAD improves design efficiency; CAM improves manufacturing efficiency; CIM integrates all aspects of production.

1 So its costs (notably fixed costs) are spread over maximum output, so that resources are used to their maximum efficiency.

8.3 Controlling stock

After studying this section you should be able to:

- *explain stock-related costs faced by a firm*
- *describe how a firm can optimise its stock control*

Controlling operations

AQA	M2
EDEXCEL	M2
OCR	M2, M3
WJEC	M5
NICCEA	M3

Firms must hold sufficient stocks of items for a number of reasons.

Item	Reason	Costs of zero stock
Raw materials and work in progress	To meet production requirements	Idle time (worker and machine); knock-on effect of delayed production
Finished goods	To meet customer demand	Loss of goodwill and orders; financial penalties for missing deadlines
Consumables, spares, equipment	To support sales and production	Idle time (worker and machine); delayed production

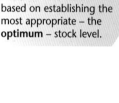

Efficient stock control is based on establishing the most appropriate – the **optimum** – stock level.

If stocks are too high, unnecessary **holding costs** will be incurred: these include storage and stores operation costs, interest charges on the capital tied up in the stocks, insurance costs, and any costs of deterioration, obsolescence or theft. Costs of having zero stock are outlined above: these costs also apply to a firm holding too little stock. The firm faces the **opportunity cost** of being without stock, i.e. the opportunity of being able to meet an order and, possibly, losing the customer to a competitor.

Firms will need to **manage** their stock efficiently. The oldest stock will normally be used first (stock **rotation**), and stock **wastage** must be minimised.

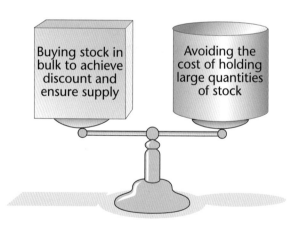

Figure 8.3 *The purchasing balancing act*

Stock control calculations

There are four critical control levels used in keeping optimum stock.

1 Reorder quantity (Economic Order Quantity: EOQ)

$$EOQ = \sqrt{\frac{2od}{h}}$$

where o = ordering cost of item,
d = (annual) demand for item, and
h = holding cost of 1 unit per annum

If, therefore, the annual demand for an item is 5,000 units, its ordering cost is £80, and the annual unit holding cost is £5:

$$EOQ = \sqrt{\frac{2(80)(5,000)}{5}} = 400 \text{ units}$$

This EOQ calculation is based on a number of assumptions, i.e. that:

- there is a constant demand for the stock item
- there is a constant lead time (time between placing an order and receiving it)
- stock-outs are not acceptable
- costs of making an order are constant, regardless of order size
- costs of holding stock vary proportionately with the amount of stock held.

2 Reorder level

Maximum lead time = ordering time + delivery time + inspection/storage time

This level triggers a reordering stock, and is calculated by:

reorder level = rate of usage × maximum lead time

3 Minimum stock

To illustrate calculating reorder level and minimum stock, assume maximum stock is 10,000, weekly usage between 2,200 and 1,800, and delivery time between 4 and 8 weeks. Reorder level is 17,600 (2,200 X 8) and minimum stock is 17,600 – (2,000 X 6) = 5,600 units.

This is the **buffer** stock level, and is calculated by:

minimum stock = reorder level – (average usage X average lead time)

4 Maximum stock

This is a warning that the stock level is at a maximum:

maximum stock = reorder level + reorder quantity
– (minimum usage × minimum lead time)

Stock control **charts** may be constructed, to show these elements visually.

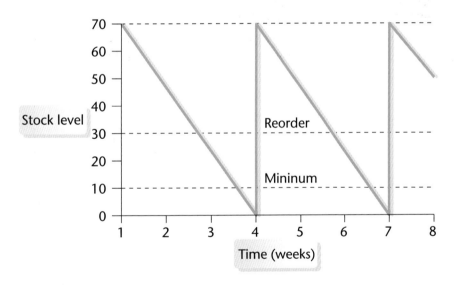

Figure 8.4 Stock control chart

1 Why does a retailer such as Tesco need efficient stock control?

2 What costs are associated with a firm's stocks?

2 Purchasing cost; opportunity cost; holding costs (wastage, obsolescence, insurance, etc.).

1 Minimise stockholding costs; ensure stock available for customers as and when required.

8.4 Quality management

After studying this section you should be able to:

- *describe why quality control is important in business*
- *assess the value of following a benchmarking process*
- *explain how quality initiatives such as TQM influence business*

LEARNING SUMMARY

Developing quality

AQA	M2
EDEXCEL	M2
OCR	M2, M3
WJEC	M5
NICCEA	M3

Quality assurance seeks to ensure that customer satisfaction is achieved by agreeing and implementing quality standards throughout the organisation. This is achieved through quality management.

An example of how quality assurance is achieved is through **quality circles**. These consist of employee groups with a common interest, who meet to discuss quality-related work issues. The group consists mainly of colleagues from the same production area, though it may also include specialists from related areas such as the Sales and Quality departments. Closely linked to the **Kaizen** philosophy (see page 122), quality circles can improve product quality, and increase employee productivity and employee morale through involvement.

Quality control

> Efficient quality control depends on efficient random **sampling** of the manufactured items.

Quality control is an important feature of production control through its identification and scrapping of unsuitable output. Traditionally carried out by quality control inspectors, a recent trend has been for employees to adopt a **self-checking** approach: this is an example of the **people-centred management** philosophy, and that quality is the responsibility of all employees.

The purpose of quality control is to ensure that standards are being maintained at least, especially where traditional flow-line production is used. It achieves this by concentrating on:

> Quality control **charts** can be used to plot the percentage of defective items made over time: increases can be seen, and remedial action taken.

- **preventing** problems from arising in the first place
- **detecting** quality problems before the goods reach the customer
- **correcting** problems and procedures
- **improving** quality to meet improved customer expectations.

Specific costs associated with quality control include the costs of:

- materials scrapped
- labour time wasted
- inspection and measurement
- rectifying poor workmanship
- lost customers due to defective products
- training employees to monitor output quality.

Benchmarking

> Benchmarking can be traced back to the 1980s in the USA: the Xerox Corporation sent a team to Japan to study why Canon could sell its photocopiers at a lower price than Xerox was managing to make its own copiers for.

Benchmarking measures a firm's production (or other activity) against the most competitive industry performance standards: it seeks out better or best practice from other organisations, and managers compare this practice to that of the firm. By doing this, the firm focuses more on external competition, rather than on its annual internal progress, to ensure it remains competitive.

Benchmarking may operate at various levels, it:

- provides basic 'market intelligence' information for the firm
- keeps management abreast of developments
- encourages the firm to adopt 'best practice'.

According to a 1994 survey by Coopers and Lybrand, about 4 in 5 companies in *The Times* Top 1000 were using benchmarking, mainly in the areas of customer service, manufacture, human resources and information services.

By using benchmarking, more realistic targets can be set; staff should become more motivated through involvement and teamwork; and management is quickly made aware of the firm's competitive disadvantage. Its limitations include:

- the difficulty of choosing a suitable benchmark 'partner'
- obtaining accurate benchmark information about the partner's performance
- the problem of selecting appropriate performance measures.

Quality initiatives

AQA	M2
EDEXCEL	M2
OCR	M2, M3
WJEC	M5
NICCEA	M3

This extract from Sainsbury's annual review 1999 is a good illustration of how organisations are showing an increasing awareness of the importance of quality at all stages of their operations and involvement with the outside world.

Our objectives

To provide shareholders with good financial returns by focusing on customers' needs, adding value through our expertise and innovation, and investing for future growth.

To provide unrivalled value to our customers in the quality of the goods we sell, in the competitiveness of our prices and in the range of choice we offer.

To achieve efficiency of operation, convenience and customer service in our stores, thereby creating as attractive and friendly a shopping environment as possible.

To provide a working environment where there is a concern for the welfare of each member of staff, where all have opportunities to develop their abilities and where each is well rewarded for their contribution to the success of the business.

To fulfil our responsibilities by acting with integrity, maintaining high environmental standards, and contributing to the quality of life of the community.

There are a number of quality initiatives that an organisation may implement.

A criticism made of the ISO 9000 system is that it can be possible for a firm to set up and 'achieve' low quality standards.

The International Standards Organisation (ISO) 9000 (formerly British Standard 5750)

This is a certification of quality management. It sets specifications for a quality framework, requiring firms to document procedures in a quality manual, and to evaluate their quality management systems. ISO 9000 is associated with design, manufacture, installation and final inspection.

An example of the TQM approach is the idea of 'zero defects', which encourages employees to develop a commitment to accurate work: there may also be financial rewards for achieving zero defects.

Total Quality Management (TQM)

This seeks to establish a 'quality culture' that assures the quality of work of all staff at all stages of production and sale. Associated with quality circles and emphasising the importance of after-sales service, it emphasises the 'get it right first time' philosophy.

> Firms nowadays adopt a quality culture based on the belief that it is better to get the job done correctly in the first place than to incur the costs and delays associated with failure.
>
> **KEY POINT**

Progress check

1 What will a firm's quality control system concentrate on?
2 What are the key differences between ISO 9000 and TQM?

2 ISO is systems- and procedures-based; TQM focuses on the 'get it right first time' approach.
1 Prevention; detection; correction; improvement.

Sample questions and model answers

1

(a) What is meant by 'just-in-time' production? [3]

(b) Outline briefly the benefit to be gained by firms from using this approach. [5]

> The examiner expects a definition plus a brief expansion, but make sure you place JIT in the context of mass production.

(a) 'Just-in-time' is associated with mass (or 'flow') production and is where stockholding is reduced to amounts required to just meet production demand. Tight delivery schedules are set, which may involve delivering the stock only hours or even minutes before it is needed.

> The question states that only a brief answer is required.

(b) A company should find that its cash flows are improved because less stock is held, and wastage, obsolescence and the other stockholding costs are reduced. The customer gains from lower prices since the company can be more price-competitive; the company's sales and market share should therefore increase.

2

'Total Quality Management (TQM) is the responsibility of every member of a firm'
What is TQM? To what extent does achieving TQM rely on teamwork throughout the firm? [8]

> The examiner will expect you to distinguish between the 'get it right first time' TQM approach and the more systems- and procedure-based approach of ISO 9000.

The Total Quality Management philosophy seeks to involve all the employees of an organisation in a continuing attempt to understand, meet and then exceed the expectations of the organisation's clients. It requires all members of the organisation to ensure that – at all stages of the production (or service) process – quality is achieved. It therefore sets out to establish a quality framework within which the organisation will operate.

> The question does not specify a type of organisation. It is worth giving specific examples in your answer.

To achieve total quality, employees must identify and analyse several factors, such as client needs. In addition, each member of the organisation must realise and accept that the work he or she carries out relates to another user in the organisation. These other users can also be thought of as 'clients'. For example, an assembly worker will be making a product which is then operated on by the assembly worker's colleague, or 'client': in turn, this employee may liaise with his/her supervisor who is also a client. Members of the organisation's management are therefore also clients, and they in turn have their own clients within the organisation (for example, when delegating tasks).

The acceptance of one's colleagues as clients therefore requires effective teamwork to take place. All employees must work together, with shared aims and goals in mind. This team effort is reinforced in TQM through, for example, the operation of 'quality circles' of people who have a shared interest in some aspect of the organisation's activities.

Practice examination question

1 Read the extract and answer **all** parts of the question which follows.

> *Polar Ices*
>
> Polar Ices has a small share of the West Country ice cream market. Its biggest selling line is a range of ice lollies. These are very profitable, though the extreme seasonality of the sales causes many operational problems.
>
> At present the company copes with the summer peak by building up stocks earlier in the year. This is necessary because the factory only has the 5 capacity to produce 140,000 units per month. Now the managing director is considering changing to a Just-in-Time production system. He believes that enough will be saved from the cash tied up in stock to pay for new equipment and extra temporary workers.
>
> *Polar Ices Ltd: Ice Lolly Sales 1999*
>
>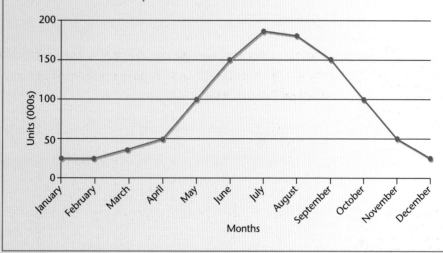

(a) (i) Explain why Polar Ices needs to build up stocks in the early part of the year. [4]

  (ii) State and explain **three** likely effects of the company building up stocks. [6]

(b) (i) Explain the meaning of the term 'Just-in-Time' production (line 7). [3]

  (ii) Discuss whether Polar Ices should switch to 'Just-in-Time' production. [8]

(c) The managing director has thought about batch production of chocolate in the winter months. Would you advise him to do this? Justify your answer. [9]

AQA Specimen Unit 2 Q2

Practice examination answers

1 (a) Price increases by 2/30 = 6.7%; income falls by 4/60 (= 2/30) = 6.7%. PED is therefore 1, meaning that the % change in demand cancels out the % change in price. [2]

(b) The firm's demand curve would shift to the right (a change in demand), with more being demanded at any price the firm charges. The firm is likely to produce more, even at the same price, which may lead to economies of scale. Depending on the elasticity of demand (which can vary according to price levels), the firm may try increasing its prices to see whether sales hold up. The competitor may have been forced to increase price, e.g. due to increased cost of raw materials, and so the firm may also face this at a later date. If the competitor has, as a result of increased prices, also increased the quality, the firm may decide to respond in kind. [9]

(c) The rise in total disposable income may, depending on the price-elasticity of the product, lead to an increased total demand. Since chocolate is not a relatively expensive item, and the price currently charged for its bar (30p to 32p) suggests that it is not a high-quality item, it is likely to be income-elastic. The firm will have to share the benefits of increased sales with its competitors: much depends on how the nature of the firm's market (e.g. age of purchasers) is affected by the rise in incomes. [6]

(d) The effect will depend to a large extent on how successful the campaign was, and how strongly chocolate was featured as part of it. If the campaign is directed towards a particular group (e.g. the young), its effect will depend on how important this group is to the firm's products. The firm will need to react if sales are affected. It might seek to diversify in the same way that tobacco companies have done; it might seek to change its image or its target market; it could change how it promotes the products; it could alter the product mix in an attempt to minimise the effect of the campaign. [11]

2 (a) The supply curve is vertical, which indicates a perfectly inelastic supply at level q1. Since we are examining a sporting event, the supply of tickets is probably fixed by the stadium's seating capacity. [3]

(b) The graph shows that, at maximum price, demand (quantity demanded = q2) is greater than supply (maximum supply level of q1). This results in a shortage of tickets (q2 minus q1). Since demand is greater than supply, some people will be prepared to pay above face value for the tickets, creating a 'black market'. [3]

(c) One way of allocation is to use the 'first come, first served' approach commonly found in sporting and other events where there is a limited number of tickets (supply). An alternative is to limit each buyer to, say, 2 tickets each: this is a form of rationing. [6]

(d) Governments choose to interfere in markets in order to regulate them. For example, the privatisation of the old state monopolies has led in some cases to the creation of privatised monopolies, which might exploit consumers without government intervention. Governments might choose to interfere in order to protect home-based industries through the use of tariffs, quotas or subsidies: examples can be seen in the Single Market (e.g. the Common Agricultural Policy and the Common External Tariff). [6]

Chapter 2 Business organisations

1 The legal status remains that of an incorporated association; the private company still has the power to enter contracts and to take (and to defend) legal action in its own name. The main differences that a change in status to a PLC will bring are in the disclosure of information and financial trading.

It is likely that the change in status will bring about a change in size (an increase), so greater economies of scale become possible. Economies of scale will make the firm more competitive: for example, it may be able to pass on lower costs through lower selling prices, thereby increasing its market share. The directors will need to be aware that diseconomies of scale may also occur.

As the company grows, the directors will find that they must disclose more of the company's financial information to the Companies Registration Office. Growth is likely because the PLC will be able to offer its shares for sale to the general public: it requires a minimum £50,000 share capital anyway. By doing this, the directors will see an increasing division between ownership and control: takeover bids become more likely through the PLC's shares being available on the Stock Exchange, and the additional information now available about the PLC may also interest potential buyers.

The directors will therefore have to balance the potential advantages of becoming a PLC – more capital which is easier to obtain, and economies of scale – with the disadvantages of disclosing further information, the loss of control, possible takeover bids, the 'short-termism' of the stock market, and drawbacks such as slower communication that can result from increasing in size. [10]

2 (a) A business franchise is a licensing arrangement between the owner of a product or service (the franchisor) and the person wishing to sell the product/service (the franchisee). The franchisee receives permission from the franchisor to make and/or distribute the franchisor's product and use the trade name and expertise, in return for (typically) paying a fee based on sales and/or time. [2]

(b) The person is provided with a nationally recognised and saleable product or service (e.g. McDonald's, Prontaprint, Thornton's); professional support is available from the franchisor in terms of advertising/marketing, shop layout, employee training, etc.; and the franchisee, by taking out the franchise, only has to commit a certain amount of capital (this tends to be less than if the franchisee was setting up in business independently). For example, a franchisee only has to commit between 25% and 40% of the total purchase price of a McDonald's franchise (source: McDonald's, 1999). [6]

(c) From the franchisor's viewpoint, expansion is possible without a high level of capital investment being required (the franchisee contributes much of this). The franchisor is also working with someone who is highly motivated to make the operation a success, since the franchisee's income depends on selling the product or service. The success of existing franchises also makes it easier for the franchisor to sell any unsold franchises. [4]

(d) The benefits of independent sole trader ownership include freedom of operation with sole decision-making, and sole ownership of the rewards (profits). The loss to the sole trader through taking on a franchise include: the loss of control over marketing, products, etc; the loss of some profit to the franchisor (royalty payments); and dependence on the franchisor, who is the more powerful party in the agreement. [6]

3 The private sector is influenced by the profit motive, whereas the public sector has traditionally focused more on providing services to the whole community.

Education and health have not normally been associated with a profit motive, but there is recent evidence to suggest that some organisations are able to run schools and hospitals, and to make a profit from this.

Education and health have been regarded and supplied as 'free' services, e.g. compulsory state education, the NHS being free at the point of service. There is a thriving private sector in both areas – independent schools, BUPA – which claim to offer a 'better' service to those who are willing and able to pay for it. The profit motive is also an efficient way of allocating resources. If, however, privately owned education and health became the norm, there is evidence (e.g. from the USA) that the few might benefit to the disadvantage of many who may not be able to afford these services. [8]

4   The workers in the pig-rearing industry will probably suffer as the demand for pork and bacon falls, and that for other meat or alternative foods rises. This is likely if the controls result in a restriction on the number (therefore the supply) of pigs available: the price of other meat and foodstuffs becomes more competitive. The owners of pig farms will also be affected, by a fall in their profits as their sales are reduced (although unit selling price may increase, to counter this).

If demand falls, suppliers to the pig farmers will in turn find that their sales are reduced. Local communities may also be affected, as local unemployment rises and expenditure falls. [8]

Chapter 3 Structure and growth

1   (a) There is a relatively narrow span of control of four subordinates, at each level of the hierarchy. As a result, there are up to five levels in parts of the hierarchy, representing only 32 employees below the Managing Director. This suggests there may be over-long lines of formal communication through the chain of command, leading to potential problems created by the 'distance' between top and bottom in the hierarchy. A narrow span of control is also sometimes associated with bureaucratic procedures, autocratic and impersonal management, and poor levels of morale.

There is a discrepancy between Marketing and other departments. There are additional levels in Marketing, which is surprising given the nature of the business. A soft drinks manufacturer will almost certainly operate flow-line production, and the Operations department would normally have a longer hierarchy with a plant manager for each site when compared with Marketing, given the fact that Fizzy Drinks plc is based on five sites. [8]

(b) There could be several reasons for the conflict between the managers. For example, a personality clash may exist (solutions include team-based training or a reallocation of duties); there seems to be lack of personal contact, given the use of memos rather than 'phone calls or face-to-face discussions (solutions include reviewing formal communication systems, e.g. number of, and attendance at, meetings). Another reason may be that, due to poor formal or informal communications, the managing director is not aware of this problem (solution again may be to review communication); if he/she is aware, this indicates poor leadership (solution, Board to review appointments and leadership). Another reason may be that the firm is over-stretched, being based on five sites. Management will have to review its location, and its internal structure (e.g. consider removing Research and Development from under the control of Operations). [10]

(c) Reorganisation could take place as follows. The firm may become task-based, and therefore operate using a matrix-based structure rather than its present, traditional, role-based one. It could base its organisation on its products (it is 'producing a range of soft drinks'), or it may base the restructuring on geographical area since it operates on more than one site. Whatever restructuring format is adopted is likely to increase the importance of the Operations element, given the nature of the firm (see (a) above). [8]

Chapter 4 External influences

1 (a) The British government will wish to see jobs remain through Ford and Vauxhall staying in the UK, and new jobs created by Toyota setting up manufacture in the UK. These companies do not only provide direct employment: by also purchasing items they require – for manufacture, food and drink for employees, etc. – from component and other firms, they support employment elsewhere. A fall in employment, e.g. through Ford or Vauxhall moving production overseas, increases demand on the 'public purse' (unemployment and other benefits being paid). At the same time, the government's tax income – from corporation (profits) tax, and income tax from employees - would fall. If the companies move production overseas, this will also adversely affect the UK's balance of payments position through both increasing imports and losing exports. [10]

(b) Society is becoming more and more aware of environmental issues associated with vehicles: examples include the concern over vehicle exhaust adding to problems of 'global warming', and health-related problems such as asthma being associated with vehicle emissions. These companies will therefore take greater account of environmental issues when designing and manufacturing vehicles, and when marketing them.

The mission statements and strategic objectives are likely to reflect the companies' acceptance of the importance of environmental concerns. More will be spent on research and development of 'cleaner' engines, and on cars that are more economical and 'environmentally-friendly' to operate. The greater awareness of the effect of vehicles on the environment will be reflected in a changed demand for the type of vehicle sold: more consumers will demand models that do less harm to the environment. This will influence how the companies adapt their marketing strategies to meet this changing demand. [10]

2 Consumers are protected from, for example: faulty goods, unhealthy food, short measure, misleading advertising, and unfair credit trading. The main reason for this is that the consumer is not in an equal relationship with the seller of goods/services, who is normally in a stronger position. The government, therefore, seeks to provide consumer protection by creating laws to that effect. Although this legislation may be regarded by some entrepreneurs as interference in commercial activities, most businessmen and women accept that their firms can also benefit from complying with consumer protection. Efficient firms accept that the extra costs resulting from obeying consumer legislation may be offset by the benefits from increased positive reputation and image. [6]

3 (a) There are social costs associated with transport, including pollution, noise, and general disruption to the life of a local community, and the council may be hoping to reduce these costs. There are also direct financial costs to the council, including road repairs and action to prevent accidents. [4]

(b) Transport firms may use the argument of having to meet higher costs, which they would then pass on to their users (and eventually to the public) in the form of higher prices. Deliveries may also slow down, and - if demand for their services moves elsewhere - jobs may be lost. Another argument they may use is that they are paying taxes for the use of the road, so any ban is unfair.

4 Installing ICT systems takes time and commits a firm to substantial costs. In the immediate term, the old and new systems are often run concurrently, leading to increased overheads. In addition, consultants will need to be employed; the installation of the system can be disruptive; and retraining and, in some cases redundancy, can negatively affect staff morale.

In the longer term, the improved speed of ICT systems in the areas of storing, retrieving, manipulating and transmitting data and information is likely to bring cost-saving and efficiency benefits to the firm.   [6]

Chapter 5 Accounting and finance

1 (a) (i) £8.00: workings £20 − (£2 + £8 + £2)

(ii) 37,500 quantity: workings £300,000 / £8
£750,000 (37,500 x £20) sales revenue

(iii) 42,500 (80,000 − 37,500) margin of safety

(iv) Unit variable cost is £12; unit fixed cost is £300,000 / 80,000 = £3.75
Unit standard cost = £12 + £3.75 = £15.75   [12]

(b) Numerical factors: Courtmills has the 20,000 spare capacity required; there is a contribution of £1 per sweater (£13 less £12 unit costs) which will cover the cost of the machine. It will therefore break even with the order.

Non-numerical factors: there is a benefit from using the spare capacity (e.g. fixed costs are spread over more output); it may lead to additional work for the firm; the firm may be able to make effective future use of the new machine. However, the 'own label' product will compete with Courtmills' products; and other customers may find out and expect lower prices.   [20]

(c) (i) GP £820,000 so margin is 58.6% (£820,000 as % of £1,400,000)

(ii) NP £820,000 − £650,000 = £170,000: margin is 12.1%

(iii) Net assets (2.5 + 0.7 − 0.3) = capital employed (1.6 + 1.3) = £2,900,000: net profit £170,000: ROCE = £170,000 as % of £2,900,000 = 5.9%   [6]

(d) (i) Current ratio = 2.3 : 1 (0.7 : 0.3) which is above the 'rule of thumb' figure of 2 : 1. The company is in a strong position to meet short-term debts as they fall due.

(ii) Gearing = 0.55 (55%) calculated by 1.6 compared to 2.9 (1.6 + 1.3). The company is therefore highly geared. Interest payments are probably not excessive at this figure (although it depends in practice on the type of industry).   [8]

2 (a) Using the straight-line depreciation method, annual depreciation is (£70,000 − £3,500) = £66,500 / 5 = £13,300 per annum per machine. There are two machines, so the total annual depreciation charge is £26,600. The company could also use the reducing balance method: this tends to give higher amounts for depreciation in the early years of ownership, which may more accurately reflect the market value of the asset. These earlier higher depreciation figures under this method initially reduce net profit compared with the straight line

method's effect on profit: this is compensated by lower depreciation in later years (showing a higher net profit). The total net profit over the life of the machines will be the same regardless of method, once the machines are disposed of. [12]

(b) (i) Jan   Feb
         (160)   (22)

(ii) A regular negative cash flow can be seen, particularly in November, December and January. After February, the situation does not improve – it deteriorates (the March figure is (44) and the April figure is (71)). The firm therefore faces a serious financial/liquidity problem, with payments outstripping receipts from sales.

It can try to control working capital more efficiently (e.g. factor the debts, control stock, agree new credit terms with suppliers, review credit arrangements with debtors); it can take out an overdraft or short-term loan. In the longer term, the firm must review its products: e.g. why is there a fall-off in sales during March and April (soft toys are a seasonal business, but sales should be higher pre-Christmas)? [10]

Chapter 6 Human resource management

1 (a) (i) 'Flexible working' refers to when employees are not working exclusively doing one job: working methods are changed.

      (ii) 'Rationalisation' here refers to the restructuring and reorganisation of a company, with the view of improving communications and reducing costs. [4]

   (b) The results of this increased feeling of job insecurity will directly and indirectly affect firms. A direct effect will be a drop in morale, which will be reflected in falling productivity per employee. Linked to this negative working attitude may be increased levels of absenteeism and accidents, further affecting output and morale. As a result, labour turnover may increase. An indirect effect may be a reduced aggregate demand level in the economy, affecting the demand for firms' goods and services: this translates into lower sales and profits, affecting investment and general business confidence. [7]

   (c) A company will seek to overcome this by developing a new – or reviewing an existing – workforce plan. It will explore how it can develop existing employees, as well as considering how best to replace these employees as they leave. The methods and extent of training will also need to be reviewed, with HRM staff exploring the relevance of, and balance between, on-the-job and off-the-job forms that are available. Whilst existing staff will not be replaced overnight by new, skilled employees, the company will still benefit from examining its recruitment policies, in order to ensure that new recruits are suitably skilled. [9]

   (d) Writers on motivation theory accept that pay is a factor in motivation. Early theorists such as F W Taylor believed that high pay acted as the prime motivator, and many women returning to the workplace may see the pay packet as the most important factor in their return.

   However, theorists from Elton Mayo onwards have drawn attention to the importance of good human relations at work. Many have argued that work can help satisfy a range of people's needs. For example, the work of Abraham Maslow can be used to argue that Asda, by adopting the 'shift swap' scheme, is giving its employees the opportunity to achieve higher-level needs (social, self-esteem and self-actualisation) outside working hours: the likely co-operation required in running such a scheme suggests that this co-operation, together with companionship and friendship, helps employees meet these needs during work as well. Frederick Herzberg separated needs into 'motivators' and 'hygiene factors'. The hygiene factors such as pay and working conditions will be met through working for Asda and the Midland Bank: motivators such as recognition and achievement also seem to be being met by the schemes outlined.   [10]

Chapter 7 Marketing

1 (a) Costs that, in the short run, change as output changes. Examples related to Table 1 could be wages of sewing machine operatives, and cotton or synthetic materials from which the shirts are made.   [4]

(b) (i) Break-even level of output is defined as that output at which the firm is making neither a profit nor a loss, i.e. where total revenue = total costs.
Total fixed cost = 400,000 x £2.91 = £1,164,000
Unit contribution = £16 – (£3.00 + £0.60 + £2.80) = £9.60

Break-even = £ 1,164,000 / £9.60 = 121,250 shirts

(ii) Margin of safety is defined as the difference between the current level of production/sales and the break-even level.
= 145,000 – 121,250 = 23,750 shirts   [10]

(c) Smythe wishes to concentrate on 'the lower-priced market segment'. In this context, a 'segment' is a part of the market which can be separated from the rest on the basis of some consumer characteristic (such as price/income). The evidence from Table 2 is that the lower-priced segment of £4 to £6 is by far the largest market segment, and therefore Smythe has the opportunity to be successful. Its financial success, however, depends largely on whether it can cut its costs to meet the lower selling price. The company will also have to take into account that, even if sales increase (and current production capacity allows the firm to almost treble its present output), unit profit and contribution margins will be far lower than at present.

From the earlier calculations, variable costs total over £9, well above the top selling price of £6 in the new segment. A positive contribution must be made, and therefore – to sell at a price of £6 – Smythe must cut variable costs to below this figure. One obvious saving is through buying cheaper materials, which should prove acceptable for the lower-priced shirt market. It is also likely that Smythe will have to (and be able to) cut unit labour costs: this can be achieved by the company increasing production and using labour and machinery more efficiently, gaining from economies of scale.

Other influences on the company's change of strategy include: how the price elasticity of demand varies between the two market segments; the effect on current production and marketing approaches – for example, a change of image, brand name and packaging will be required; competitor reaction to the company's new strategy; and whether the existing distribution channels will still be suitable. The success of the strategy also depends on how the level of importing/exporting affects the company. A change in the value of the £ against the euro and other major currencies will affect the degree of overseas competition and the costs of imported materials.

In conclusion, given the existing variable costs it seems unlikely that Smythe can make adequate contribution and therefore profits.   [15]

Chapter 8 Productive efficiency

1 (a) (i) Polar Ices operates in a seasonal market: it therefore needs to balance its supply of its stocks with the peaks of demand (in the summer months). It will need to be able to react to high sales, which are impulse-led: the way to do this is to maintain adequate stock of finished goods. The firm will wish to even out its production process in order to maintain a steady production, which affects business issues such as employment, stock control and ordering.

(ii) Stock 'ties up' cash, which may lead to problems of liquidity for Polar Ices. The firm also faces high costs of stockholding (e.g. storage/rent, and power for the freezers). Polar Ices may also face the cost of having to destroy stock, e.g. due to freezer breakdown or through lack of demand.   [10]

(b) (i) This term refers to holding a zero buffer stock, relying on the supplier to deliver the necessary items 'just-in-time' to meet the manufacturer's order.

(ii) By doing so, Polar Ices' storage costs of raw materials will be reduced, releasing cash for the extra equipment and staff mentioned in the question. A 'just-in-time' approach lets a firm such as Polar Ices respond more quickly to market changes: it will also not be left holding stock that has deteriorated, and therefore cannot be used. Polar Ices will, however, need to review how its staff are to be utilised effectively if this change is implemented.   [11]

(c) A change such as this will require staff training, since chocolate seems to be a new product for the firm. Additional capital expenditure (e.g. buying new machines) may also be needed, which may require additional long-term finance. Batch production probably suits Polar Ices' present production processes, and since the market for chocolate is likely to be less seasonal than for ice cream, this may reduce storage problems.   [9]

Index